WATT POTTERY

A Collector's Reference with Price Guide

Dennis Thompson
& W. Bryce Watt

Schiffer Publishing Ltd

77 Lower Valley Road, Atglen, PA 19310

DEDICATION

W.I. "Ike" Watt was born and raised in Roseville, Ohio. He was the son and grandson of potters. He worked in pottery in some capacity all his life, starting at a very young age. His family, pottery and education were his whole life. In his later years, his dream was to write a book about his family pottery. On January 1st, 1988, this dream became a reality with his small book, *Collectibles*, which he marketed himself from home. This gave him a great sense of satisfaction. On February 26, 1989, Ike died leaving behind a great legacy. He is sadly missed by family and friends.

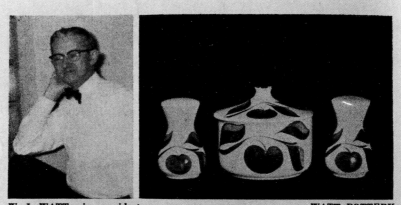

W. I. WATT, vice president ....WATT POTTERY

Watt Pottery (Space 539)

A broad sweep of new items is to be shown, including casseroles, servers, pitchers, mugs and salad bowls; prices are to be promotional. Typical item is four piece range set (see photo): salt and pepper shakers, and pint-size grease jar with lid. Retail is $2.25. Crooksville, Ohio.

"Ike" Watt doing what he did best - selling Watt pottery. *Reprinted from the Crockery and Glass Journal*, December, 1958.

Published by Schiffer Publishing, Ltd.
77 Lower Valley Road
Atglen, PA 19310
Please write for a free catalog.
This book may be purchased from the publisher.
Please include $2.95 postage.
Try your bookstore first.

We are interested in hearing from authors with book ideas on related subjects.

Acknowledgments

The authors would like to thank the following people for allowing their collections to be photographed for this book:

Don and Becky Alexander
Jon and Judy Bang
Bob and Danelle Berecz
Betty Blair
Larry and Kay Bobbitt
Patrick and Molly Busby
Warren and Kay Chapman
Jim & Christy Hogue
Debby Rees
Molly Schroeder
Ken and Sandee Schmitt
Tom and Chris Schmitt
Ina Seaver
Karen Stern
Dick & Linda Watt
Larry and Jackie Watt
Ken Yurkewecz
Eva Zeisel

The authors extend thanks to many others who contributed in different ways:

Tracy and Jill Cigrand for always knowing we would do this book.

Shirley Dickson of the Zanesville Times Recorder.

Shelly Loomis for her help sorting and captioning photographs.

Gwen Petechik of Dodd Camera in Fairview Park for all of her photo-processing.

Jim Schulte and Lori Hinterleiter of *Purinton Pastimes* for their help researching Esmond ware.

We would like to express our very special appreciation to the former decorators of the Watt Pottery:

Ruth Fitzer, Betty Ford, Glenna Gossman, Hazel McCray, Joy McGrath, and Jackie Sherrick.

Glossary

Arbor: A round plate attached to the end of a shaft. The arbor spins with the shaft, and a piece of ware to be decorated is placed on the arbor. The arbor used by the bander was powered by a motor, while the arbor used by the decorators was simply spun by hand.

Jiggering: A semi-automated process for forming pottery. This is a mechanized version of the old potter's wheel. Wet clay is placed in a rotating mold (sometimes called a "buck") and a blade is lowered onto the clay while it spins. The mold forms the outside of the piece, and the blade (called a "shoe") forms the inside. More modern versions have several molds for each operator.

Kiln: The hot oven-like area where the dried ware is fired to completion. Watt ware is fired to over 2100 degrees F. A "periodic kiln" must be filled with ware, and then sealed and heated. After cooling, all of the ware is unloaded at once. In a "continuous kiln", the ware is carried through the heating and cooling process on heat-resistant railroad cars. This type of kiln never shuts off except for maintenance. "Muffle" and "down-draft" kilns are specific types of periodic kilns.

Lip: The outer edge of a bowl, if it is flared in profile. If the bowl also has a shoulder, the lip is on top of the shoulder. Many of the more modern Watt pieces have no lips.

Mark: Commonly called a "bottom mark". As it refers to Watt pottery, a mark is molded into the bottom of the ware and may be embossed (raised) or impressed. Most Watt marks are impressed and contain the words, "Oven Ware U.S.A.".

Nappy: An English term for a low, rounded bowl. It is a term used somewhat loosely, but the bowls in the Watt line which were primarily called nappies were the #04 through #07, and the #600 through #604.

Shoulder: A heavy, raised band around the outer edge of a bowl. Shoulders are found on most Watt pieces made prior to 1953. A piece with a shoulder may also have a lip on it.

Signed: A piece is considered signed if the decorator's name or initials are hand written under the glaze and fired. Signed pieces of Watt ware are rare, and are usually custom decorated.

Slip: A thin, fluid mixture of clay. Water and various minerals called "deflocculants" are added to the clay to make slip. Slip is used to cast pieces in a mold in a process called "slip-casting". Slip may also be prepared with colors to be used for decorating the ware. The casting slip in the Watt Pottery was kept in a large underground tank and pumped to the casting rooms on the second floor. The employees called it "soup".

Contents

In July, 1993, the authors reunited many of the former Watt employees at Watt Fest I, the national convention of the Watt Pottery
Collectors USA. To demonstrate their craft, several decorators
produced a series of commemorative plates to be used as door prizes.
These pie plates were decorated by Hazel McCray.

In a very short time, dozens of plates were completed by the
decorators while collectors watched. These plates were decorated by
Betty Ford.

Introduction

The Watt decorators share fond memories of the Watt Pottery. From left to right: Hazel McCray, Betty Ford, Glenna Gossman, Jackie Sherrick.

The story of the Watt Pottery is also a story of the Watt family. It began on a quiet hillside in Rose Farm, Ohio, over one hundred years ago. At one time, three generations of Watt family members worked together in the pottery. Together they operated the company which produced their ware and sold it from coast to coast.

In the early years, the Watt name was not used as the company name. The company known officially as the Watt Pottery existed from July 5th, 1922, until a disastrous fire ended production on October 4th, 1965.

The Watt Pottery made primarily dinner and kitchen ware. A small selection of garden ware was produced, but the company never ventured into the areas of art pottery or sanitary ware. The ware was designed to be inexpensive, durable and colorful. It could go from oven to table and into the refrigerator without breaking. To test the durability of the ware, W.I. Watt often took pieces home to bake in the oven, and then place directly into the refrigerator. Time after time he repeated the heating and cooling, to ensure that each batch of clay was indeed oven safe.

One aspect of the pottery's appeal is the uniqueness of each piece of the hand-decorated ware. The patterns are simple, executed with a few strokes of boldly colored glaze. The differences from piece to piece reflect the speed with which each was produced, and the hands of each decorator.

Quite a few of the Watt employees are alive and well, and living in Crooksville. Many stay in touch with each other. They all are quite amazed that the pottery which they produced by the thousands is so eagerly sought after by today's collectors. This book is their story as well.

Most of the corporate records of the Watt Pottery were lost in the 1965 fire. Fortunately, the records pertaining to the early history of the company, from 1922 to the early 1950s, were at W. I. Watt's home in Roseville. From these records we were able to reconstruct a detailed history up to about 1952. Mr. Watt's own book, *Collectibles*, was the source of much of the history during the 1950s.

A handful of catalogs from the 1950s and 1960s were kept by the Watt family. These catalogs were invaluable for helping to date the progression of the various shapes of the ware. These catalogs have been reproduced for this book at the end of chapter 2.

Very few production records survived. Fortunately, those records which we were able to find filled in many gaps in our study of the ware.

Another source of information concerning the Watt Pottery is the memories of the Watt family and the pottery's employees. In the last two years alone, several people have passed away who may have contributed to this history. The Watt Pottery closed nearly 30 years ago, and the authors felt that now was the time for a complete history of the pottery, before more information was lost.

Fire is an integral part of pottery making. Each new piece emerges from a 2000 degree baptism. But fire is also the enemy of the pottery. Like so many other potteries, the Watt Pottery ended in a blaze. The legacy of the company is the ware itself. There are certainly over 1500 different pieces of Watt ware, and perhaps as many as 2000 pieces. We have photographed over 1350 for this book...enjoy.

Chapter 1
When Eagles Flew Over Crooksville

THE WATT POTTERY COMPANY

MANUFACTURERS

"MATCHED" OVENWARE AND KITCHENWARE

GARDENWARE

STONEWARE  SPECIALTIES

William J. Watt was born November 11, 1857, in the village of McCluney, Ohio, just south of Crooksville. In 1879, William married Almeda Ransbottom. Their children were Harry, Thomas, Marion, Cora, Grayce, Gladys and Ruth. The three sons, Harry, Thomas and Marion Watt, would grow up to be the co-founders of the Watt Pottery with W.J. Watt in 1922.

At the age of 29, W.J. Watt purchased 80 acres of land in Rose Farm, Morgan County, Ohio. Coal and clay, geological partners, were found in abundance on the farm. Here Watt built a "bluebird pottery", one of many in the area. These outdoor potteries could only be worked in good weather. When the bluebirds returned each spring, it was time to begin operating again. Nestled alongside a long hill near the coal and clay veins, W.J. Watt's little pottery was named the Brilliant Stoneware Company.

The operation was all hand-worked at first, aided only by a blind horse who pulled the steel-clad, wooden wheels around in a wet-pan which ground the clay. Ware was turned on a foot-operated kick wheel. James Pitcock, George Wilson and Joe Armstrong were some of the potters who turned ware for the company. Only two commemorative pieces of ware have been identified from the Brilliant Stoneware Company.

Drying took place in a tunnel shaped dryer covered with sand and fired with coal or wood. Ware was glazed on the inside and stored until enough was turned and dried to fill the kiln. Kilns were up-draft, periodic types known as beehive kilns because of their shape. The ware was salt glazed as it was fired.

This two-handled, thirty gallon jug was made at the Brilliant Stoneware Company on August 29, 1895, by Joe Armstrong. It is over 34" high and weighs 110 lbs. It was turned in two pieces and joined together before firing. A companion jug of forty gallons capacity is known to exist.

The Brilliant Stoneware Company in Rose Farm, Ohio, c. 1890. W.J. Watt stands on the far left.

About 1890, the pottery was modernized with new buildings, a steam engine and two new kilns. One kiln was a muffle type, and the other was a center down-draft style.

The ware was sold in Ohio, Indiana and northern Kentucky by W.J. Watt's brother-in-law, Royal Conaway. Ware was shipped on the Cincinnati and Muskingham Railroad.

In 1897, the buildings burned, leaving the kilns standing. At this time, W.J. Watt sold the pottery to Benjamin Beck and he and his family moved to Roseville, Ohio.[1]

The Brilliant Stoneware Company after the fire in 1897. The kilns and drying ovens are all that remain.

Almeda Watt's brothers, Ed, Mort, Charles and Frank Ransbottom, formed the Ransbottom Brothers Pottery in 1902. They purchased the Oval Ware and Brick Company in Ironspot, Ohio, just north of Roseville. By 1906 the building covered 3 1/2 acres and employed 100 men.[2] Frank Ransbottom was the manager. Thomas Watt was the superintendent and Harry and Marion Watt worked as jiggermen. As a young boy of ten in 1918, William Iliff Watt, son of Thomas Watt, worked at the Ransbottom Brothers Pottery. His pay was 1/2 cents per hour, and he worked 10 hour days, six days a week.

The Watt and Ransbottom families, c. 1890s. The Watts are in the back row. W.J. is standing at the far left, Thomas is the third from the right and Harry is the fourth from the right.

By 1921 the Watt family had saved enough money to once again establish their own pottery. At that time, W.J. Watt purchased a pottery at Edison, Ohio, two miles west of Mount Gilead. Although details are unclear, our research suggests that the Mount Gilead Tile and Clay Works may have been the pottery W.J. Watt purchased. Sometime around 1920 this pottery changed hands and became the Florence Pottery.[3] This would indicate that the property was for sale at approximately the time W.J. Watt made his purchase. Edison is quite a distance from the Watt's family home in Roseville, however, and when the Globe Stoneware Company was offered for sale, Mr. Watt resold the pottery at Edison and purchased the old Globe Stoneware Company at 101 China Street in Crooksville.

The Globe Stoneware Company had been started in 1901 and purchased in 1912 by Zane Burley who renamed it the Burley Pottery Company. (In *Collectibles*, W.I. Watt still refers to the property as the Globe Stoneware Company). The purchase price of the property to Mr. Watt was $20,000.[4]

The property that the Watt family had purchased consisted of eight rooms, each of which was referred to as a building in the company's records,[5] but which together were contained by a brick wall, so that the overall impression from the outside was of a single building. The total area of the buildings was just under 40,000 square feet. The Globe Stoneware Company had been destroyed by a fire in 1906, and the original frame buildings were replaced with brick. Most of the buildings were listed as built in 1909 or 1911. Only the areas for storing, packing and shipping the ware were built in 1904, before the fire.

The incorporation papers for the Watt Pottery were filed on July 5, 1922. The capital stock of the corporation was listed at $50,000, divided into 500 shares of $100 each. Only 205 shares worth $20,500 were originally purchased by the Watt family: 50 shares each by Harry, Thomas, and Marion Watt, and C.L. Dawson (a son-in-law) and 5 shares by W.J. Watt.

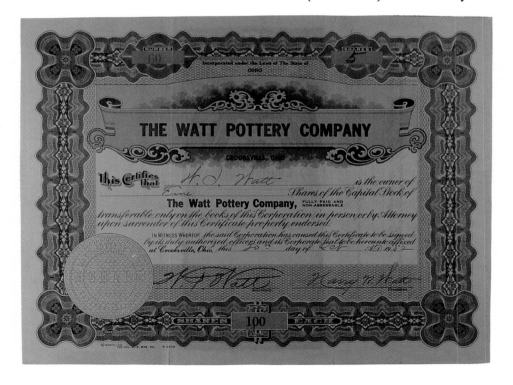

A stock certificate from the Watt Pottery.

On July 8, 1922, the first directors' meeting was held and the following officers were elected:

Leonard Dawson	President
Marion Watt	Vice President
Harry Watt	Secretary and Treasurer
Thomas Watt	General Manager

The first ware which could be called "Watt" was now being produced. This early ware was all stoneware and consisted of jars, jugs, Dutch pots, milk pans, churns, chamber pots, and mixing bowls. The ware is not marked and is very generic in nature. It is doubtful that any ware from this era could be identified.

Sales of the ware were entirely through the American Clay Products Company. This company was located in the Masonic Temple in Zanesville and was made up of all potteries in Crooksville and Roseville, Ohio, and the Logan Pottery Company, owned by Charles Adcock, in Logan, Ohio.

All principals in the American Clay Products Company were charged for their interest in the organization. The Watt Pottery's share was $4500, and the records of proceedings from 1922 indicate that Harry Watt shall "receive and hold the stock in the American Clay Products Company, which is acquired from Zane W. Burley, for the receipt of this company."[6]

Orders for wares were distributed by the agency according to the capitalization of the individual potteries.[7] No one belonging to the agency could sell wares to anyone other than the agency's buyers without the written consent of the other potteries. The American Clay Products Company was liquidated on January 1, 1926, but while it lasted, the list of officers reads like a "Who's Who" of area potters:

F.M. Ransbottom	President
A.E. Hull	1st Vice President
C.L. Adcock	2nd Vice President
Floyd Hull	Treasurer
John Burley	Assistant Treasurer
Nelson McCoy	Secretary

In December of 1922, the Dewey Council, presumably composed of workers from various local potteries, organized a strike by the workers at ten potteries in Crooksville including the Watt Pottery. They sought higher wages and recognition of the Dewey Council as the bargaining agent for the potteries' labor force.[8] After several idle days, Harry and Marion Watt began jiggering ware to meet shipping orders, and Thomas Watt glazed the ware. When enough ware to fill a kiln was ready, the entire family helped set the kiln. After firing, all would draw the kiln, and W.J. Watt and Leonard Dawson packed the ware for shipping. By the end of the month, disillusioned union members would show up at the plant two or three at a time to seek work, and all were immediately hired back. Soon a full crew was employed, and when the other pottery workers in Crooksville heard that the Watt Pottery was back in production, they started back to work also. The Dewey Council was ended.

In January, 1923, Harry Watt was authorized to borrow up to $10,000 from the Crooksville Bank for additional operating capital.[9]

A series of stock transfers left the Brush Pottery Company in control of the Watt Pottery in 1926. On December 30, 1925, Marion and Thomas Watt each purchased 18 additional shares of stock, and Harry Watt purchased 43 more. The following week, they sold all of their newly acquired stock, plus 5 shares each of their original 50 shares, to the Brush Pottery. Leonard Dawson sold all of his original 50 shares and was no longer a partner. The Brush Pottery purchased 1 share outright,

and several other shares were sold to individuals. At the January 11th annual meeting, the new stock distribution was:

Brush Pottery Co.	145 shares
Harry Watt	45 shares
Thomas Watt	45 shares
Marion Watt	45 shares
Jno. Taylor	1 share
S.M. Seright	1 share
George Brush	1 share
W.R. Baker	1 share

Harry Watt replaced Leonard Dawson as president of the company, and George Brush was elected as sales manager. A salary of $50.00 per week was approved for Mr. Brush and also for Harry, Thomas, and Marion Watt. The Brush Pottery, with 51% of the stock, essentially operated the Watt Pottery as one of their stoneware production departments. When the American Clay Products Company was liquidated in 1926, the entire output of the Watt Pottery was sold through Brush's sale organization.[10]

Later that same year, 1926, W.J. Watt - potter, founder and operator of the Brilliant Stoneware Company, and one of the founders of the Watt Pottery, died, having suffered a stroke in 1923.

In October, 1927, the construction company of Bonifant, Carr and Sagle was engaged to build additional offices and warehouses. This 7,200 square foot, two-story, brick structure cost $7,391 and was attached to the rest of the building. It was on the far right side of the pottery and featured the familiar porch and company sign seen in photographs of the pottery.

The Watt Pottery. The office addition on the right was built in 1927. The large jars on either side of the doorway are rare Brush bungalow jars.

In January, 1930, the annual report showed that the company's sales for the year of 1929 were $42,628. At the annual meeting, George Brush replaced Marion Watt as vice president of the company, and William Iliff "Ike" Watt was elected as secretary, his first office in the company. The salary for the principal officers was increased to $75.00 a week.

By January, 1931, the Watt Pottery was making enough profit that the board declared the first dividend of 5%. The company also established a charity fund by placing $100.00 into an account which was added to each year.

In March of the same year, the Brush Pottery offered to sell their 145 shares of capital stock back to the Watt Pottery for the sum of $20,000 and agreed to waive their unpaid dividend for 1930. George Brush had purchased 30 more shares of stock for himself by this time, and remained as sales manager. The Watt family was now back in complete control of their pottery. It would stay family-owned throughout the remainder of its history.

Sales of pottery were very good through the early 1930's. By mid-1932, the company's stock dividend was increased to 20%. But by the end of 1933, the economic climate in the nation had changed. The company's stock dividend had dropped to only 1%. In May, 1935, the Watt family felt a change was needed to place the company in a better market position. They decided to cease production of stoneware and to begin making oven-proof kitchen and bake ware.

W.J. Watt's brothers-in-law, the Ransbottoms, must have provided formidable competition for the stoneware market at this time. They had merged with the Robinson Clay Products Company in 1920 to form the Robinson-Ransbottom Pottery Company. By the mid-1920s, Robinson-Ransbottom, located a mere five miles north in Roseville, had become the world's largest producer of stoneware.

In retrospect, the Watt family had entered the stoneware market as its peak was approaching. By the 1930s housewives wanted more modern cookware, and dishes which could go from the oven to the table and into the icebox fit the bill. A loan of $12,000 was negotiated with the Crooksville Bank to finance the switch to the new product line.

It was during this time that the pottery's symbol, a proud eagle with wings spread over the words, "Watt Ware" and "Crooksville, Ohio" appeared on the company's letterhead in royal blue.

In 1936, potteries in Crooksville and Roseville recognized a newly formed union of laborers, ending a four month strike. The union represented workers in the Watt Pottery, Robinson-Ransbottom Pottery, Nelson McCoy Pottery, W.I. Tycer Pottery, Brush Pottery, A.E. Hull Pottery, and the Star Stoneware Company. The settlement established a minimum wage scale for twenty-three job categories. Wages ranged from $2.64 per eight-hour day for female finishers and helpers to the jiggerman's wage of $4.64 per day. Typical for the time, women were paid about 75% of a man's wages for the same job.

Through the rest of the 1930s, dividends remained low. When they were mentioned in the corporate records, they were still 1%.

In 1940, sales began increasing. That year the dividend was raised to 4%, and a bonus was paid to all employees. At the November, 1941 meeting, when the increased business was mentioned in the minutes, semi-annual bonuses for all employees were instituted. The bonuses ranged from $5.00 to $50.00 based on job classification, to be paid when the earnings of the company allowed. The general manager's salary had been raised earlier that year from $75.00 per week ($3900 annually) to an annual salary of $7500, and an additional dividend of 24% was authorized.[11]

At this writing, it is speculation as to the cause of the dramatic increase in sales in 1940. But the authors note that production records for the patterns which we call the "Early Kitchen and Oven Ware" first appear in 1940. Perhaps the ware of the late 1930s was still very ordinary in nature, even though it was oven ware.

In the early 1940s, dividends held steady at 5%, and additional quarterly dividends were paid as business allowed. The Watt Pottery began investing in war bonds during this time. In 1941 and 1942, the company invested $10,000 in war bonds and $5000 in tax savings certificates.

By October, 1942 the declared value of the capital stock was set at $200,000. In December, shareholder W.G. McConnell was elected sales manager. The following year the bylaws were ammended to allow a sixth board member, and Mr. McConnell was elected to the board.

The years 1943 through 1944 brought dividends ranging from 5% to 15%. Each year, at least $15,000 was invested in bonds and tax savings certificates. By July, 1945, the declared value of the capital stock had increased to $300,000. By the end of the war, the company had repaid all of its debts at the Crooksville Bank. The *History of Crooksville, Ohio*, written by Guy E. Crooks in 1945, stated,

> "The Watt Pottery Company has the neatest, the most modern and successfully operated stoneware plant in the Crooksville district. The Watts should all live in Crooksville. They are not only good potters, but enterprising business men and would be an asset to the citizenship of Crooksville."

This modern operation was made possible by the extensive modernization plan which took place throughout the 1940s. Production was made more efficient by adding automatic mold release systems, semi-automatic jiggering machines, and more sophisticated clay grinding and sieving operations. Ware was moved from area to area by conveyors, eliminating the need for carts pushed along the aisles. The labor force was actually reduced during this period, even as production increased.

The Watt Pottery in the 1940s.

Sometime during this period of time, the old periodic kilns were replaced with a continous operation kiln of circular design. This kiln was an Allied Engineering Company design, 55 feet in diameter on the center line. The firing chamber was 26 feet long, 11'-8" wide and 7'-2" high. Twenty six merry-go-round cars carried ware in a continous motion, 24 hours a day. The areas of the pottery were: (see sketch of floor plan)

1   Clay and glaze mixing
1A   Repair shop
2   Manufacturing building
3   Manufacturing and office
4   Allied Engineering 55' circular kiln
5   Warehouse
6   Warehouse and shipping
7   Storage and packing
8   Storage and shipping
9   Storage
10   Straw storage (for packing)
11   Clay storage

In 1948, the Watt Pottery took the major step of hiring decorators to produce hand-decorated dinner ware in floral patterns. By mid-1949 the first pattern, Rio Rose, was in production. With W.I. Watt now the sales manager, sales of the hand-decorated ware launched the company into the boom years of the 1950s.

On June 26, 1949, the Zanesville Times-Signal carried the story of the new line of Watt pottery - Rio Rose, the first freehand, decorated ware by the Watt Pottery was in production.

The decade had barely begun when disaster struck. On Friday evening, June 16, 1950, torrential rains struck Ohio from Cincinnati north to Akron. Several inches of rain fell south of Crooksville in a few hours. Moxahala Creek rose rapidly from the downpour. There had been several floods earlier in the century in Crooksville, but this one was different. The dam five miles south of town, owned by the Misco Mining Company, held for a while, allowing large amounts of water through the spillway. But around midnight one end of the dam was breached, and an eight-foot wall of water surged down Moxahala Creek into Crooksville.

Surprised residents were trapped in cars and buidings where they stood. The Watt Pottery's kiln shed boss, "Shorty" Severts, realized that the rapidly rising water presented a grave danger to

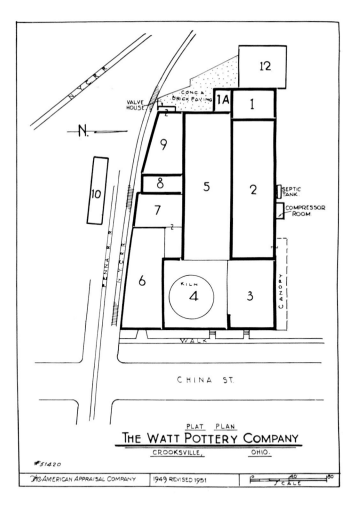

A floor plan of the Watt Pottery drawn in 1951. See text for description.

the hot kiln, so he stayed long enough to shut down the fires in the kiln thereby saving the pottery from almost certain destruction. When W.I. Watt heard of Severts' actions he told him, "Shorty, you will have a job with this company for the rest of your life".

The significance of Severts' courage and foresight was underscored by the fate of a nearby pottery. The Acme plant, operated by the A.E. Hull Pottery, had to be quickly abandonded. Before the eyes of onlookers, the kiln exploded with a terrific blast, instantly setting fire to the entire building. Firefighters were blocked by the flood waters and could only watch as the pottery burned down to the water.[12]

The next day, the fire department washed broken ware out the back door of the Watt Pottery with hoses. The cleanup took about six weeks and cost $75,000. Employees were paid their regular wages to assist in the rebuilding.

A second catastrophe struck the pottery in January, 1951, when a fire broke out in the plant burning the manufacturing area. It cost $75,000 to replace the building with an additional $50,000 worth of contents lost. The resulting two-month interruption in production was followed in the company's advertisements, as they advised potential buyers of the progress. [13]

Firemen working to save the Watt Pottery in 1951. The Brush bungalow jar were gone by then, replaced by unknown jars. These jars disappeared after the fire in 1965.

"Burned Out Area" written in Area #2. This is the section of the pottery damaged in the 1951 fire. Area #14 is warehouse space added in the early 1950's. Total floor space in the pottery was now 60,000 square feet.

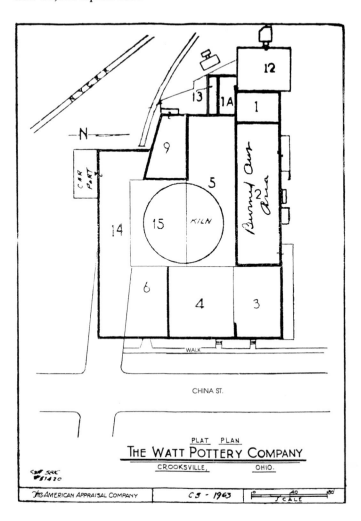

The final floor plan of the pottery with the new kiln in position in 1963. Hand written in section No. 2 is the note, "Burned out area." This is the area damaged in the 1951 fire.

The new lines of hand-decorated ware proved very popular. New patterns and additional pieces were issued year by year. The shape of the ware evolved during the 1950's from the post-war look to a sleeker, more contemporary styling. Sales for the first five months of 1953 were $215,800, equalling a yearly sales rate of over $500,000.[14]

On October 26, 1959, Thomas Watt died at the age of 77. He had been vice president of the Watt Pottery since 1926. His son, W.I. Watt, assumed the office of vice president at this time, in addition to his position of sales manager.

A larger, more modern, circular kiln was installed in 1960, bringing about a final, major change in the pottery's manufacturing capabilities. The Limoges China Company in Sebring, Ohio had gone out of business in 1956. The kiln was purchased by the Watts and dismantled brick by brick to be reassembled in Crooksville. Every week during the summer, workers drove a flat bed truck to Sebring and loaded it with more bricks. The process took about three months to complete.

The new kiln, also built by Allied Engineering, was much larger than the existing one. It was 70 feet in diameter on the center line, compared to 55 feet for the older kiln. The firing chamber was 36 feet long, and the chamber was two feet wider and over four feet taller than the old kiln. When this kiln was placed in operation, the pottery could fire more than five million pieces of ware every year.

In the accompanying sketch, the new kiln is #15. The old kiln, formerly in area #4 has been removed. Note the words

By 1960, wages had risen more than 350% over the rates set by the union agreement of 1936. Female helpers were still the lowest paid, at $1.22 per hour. The highest wages, $2.08 per hour, were paid to the shape and die maker. Interestingly, the wages paid to the decorators were among the lowest at $1.25 per hour.

Sales during the 1960s were steady at approximately $750,000 a year. In 1965 a new line, Royal Danish, was designed. Sales were expected to increase by $250,000 a year, a respectful 33% increase. But it was not to be. A disastrous fire broke out, which would bring about the end of the Watt Pottery. There are no better words to describe the fire then W.I. Watt's own description from *Collectibles*:

Then on October 4, 1965 at 10:00 p.m., a fire broke out on the second floor, burning the entire manufacturing plant, warehouse and part of the office. When coming from

Roseville, where I lived, the first sign from a distance was a spectacular pall of white, billowing smoke under-lit with angry red color of destructive flames, a twisting seething mass sharpened in contrast to the frosty black October night. I knew then that nothing could save the pottery that employed 150 people in the town of Crooksville, Ohio. The scene when I arrived no longer was a brilliant display of nature. It was transformed into an awesome holocaust. The flames were leaping and licking into the sky on the north side of the building. China Street was a tangled wet mass of fire hoses from the several fire departments answering the alarm. The firemen and the volunteers went to the danger points to arrest the most violent flames. Hot coffee and sandwiches were donated by concerned citizens, which appeared to give relief to the cold, wet firemen. At a fire, firemen are usually hampered, especially in a small town, in their activities by uncontrolled masses of curious onlookers. On that night, the citizens of Crooksville were strangely quiet. They stood in huddled groups, then there was wandering from group to group. Their talk was quiet, full of fear, full of awe of the uncontrollable forces. There were some who stood alone and watched in silence, their eyes glazed with thought of now and of the future - if their jobs were in jeopardy and if the Watt Pottery would be no more.

This setback proved to be the last. After discussions, family members decided not to continue with the business. Dispersing the assets took several years to complete. When the company was finally liquidated, W.I. Watt took a position with the Frankoma Pottery. He was the sales representative for Ohio during the remainder of the 1960s, into the early 1970s. With his knowledge of the trade and already established contacts, he became one of Frankoma's best salesmen, even though he only sold in Ohio, compared to the several-state area handled by other sales representatives.

The building which held the Watt Pottery was purchased by the GlasFloss Corporation and rebuilt. In August, 1987, the building burned again. This time it was razed to the ground, and a new structure erected.

Today, 101 China Street in Crooksville is the site of a metal, contemporary, manufacturing building. The Watt Pottery, "the neatest, most modern, and successfully operated stoneware plant in... Crooksville", is gone. Only the products of that plant, which today are collected and appreciated by many, remain.

The Glasfloss Corporation operated out of the old Watt Pottery building until 1987, when it burned for the last time. None of the building remains today.

Footnotes

1. Watt, W.I., *Collectibles*, p 1-4
2. Watt, W.I., personal notes.
3. Lehner, *Ohio Pottery and Glass: Marks and Manufacturers,* p 70.
4. Watt Pottery, records.
5. American Appraisal Company, December 20th, 1951. After rebuilding from the fire in early 1951, the Watt Pottery was formally appraised. The original date of construction of all of the rooms was noted on the appraisal.
6. Watt Pottery, Records of Proceedings, July, 1922.
7. Agreement between the Watt Pottery and The American Clay Products Company, September 1st, 1922. Zane Burley had previously signed an agreement with the American Clay Products Co. on January 23, 1918. This contract was assigned to C. L. Dawson, and thus to the Watt Pottery, during the Watt's purchase of Burley's property in July, 1922.
The American Clay Products Co. agreed to distribute orders among the potteries "in the ratio and proportion of the sales made by all such manufacturing plants respectively for the years 1917 and 1918", and that as a minimum the agency would purchase a quantity equal to 60% of each pottery's sales for these years.
W. I. Watt stated that "Orders ... were distributed from the agency according to their capitalization", and that the Watt Pottery's share was $4500. It is inferred from this that the amount of each pottery's fee was also proportioned on the amount of their output during 1917 and 1918.
8. Late 1922 was a time of labor unrest between the coal miners and their union. Local papers contained many accounts of strikes and negotiations. Coal and clay are found together in nature, and thus coal and clay workers work near, and possibly learn from, each other. The authors could find no written account of the Dewey Council other than that in *Collectibles* by W. I. Watt. Possibly the Dewey Council was only a small local attempt to organize the clay workers rather than a recognized union.

The earliest agreement the authors could locate between the Watt Pottery and the workers is dated February 19th, 1936. Even this agreement, some 14 years later, is between the Watt Pottery and "the representatives of the employees of ...(the various potteries)", not a named labor union. However, in *Collectibles*, W. I. Watt stated that this was the action of the Brotherhood of Operative Potters, and that all potteries subsequently became unionized, an action made official by the National Labor Relations Board in Cincinnati, Ohio.
9. Watt Pottery, Records of Proceedings, January, 1923.
10. More details of this interesting connection between the Watt Pottery and the Brush Pottery have not been located. Most of our information comes from the corporate records of the stock transfers, and thus is not annotated. Talks with Steve Sanford, author of *The Guide to Brush-McCoy Pottery*, and recollections of author W. Bryce Watt indicate that this was not a hostile take-over, but a fully cooperative partnership between the two potteries.
Further evidence of this is demonstrated by the fact that George Brush remained as sales manager after the dissolution of the partnership in 1931. During the time of the partnership, Thomas Watt also held a position (probably that of a foreman) in the Brush Pottery. In Chapter 29 is shown a "pair-of-bears" which was produced (probably by the Brush Pottery) in 1929 to honor Thomas Watt for some unknown event.
11. Watt Pottery, Records of Proceedings, November, 1941.
12. Zanesville News and the Zanesville Signal, June 17th, 1950.
13. Watt, W. I., *Collectibles*. Mr. Watt only mentioned an approximate date and the correct date was learned from newspaper accounts. The Watt Pottery placed advertisements in *The Crockery and Glass Journal* for several months informing the industry of the repair progress.
14. Watt Pottery, Profit and Loss Statement, May, 1953.

Chapter 2
Through The Years With Watt Ware

During its brief 43 years of operation, the Watt Pottery produced a variety of ware ranging from the basic stoneware of the 1920s, to the modern look of the last line produced, the Royal Danish line. The changes in the look of the ware can be divided into several different periods of time, as shown below:

1922 to 1935	The Stoneware Age
1935 to mid-1940s	Early Kitchen and Oven Ware
1943 to 1950	Transition Ware
1949 to 1953	Classic Patterns
1952 to 1965	Modern Patterns

STONEWARE AGE, 1922 - 1935

At the onset of production in mid-1922, the Watt Pottery began producing stoneware which was very similar to most stoneware of the period. It was simple in nature, intended for utilitarian use. The style of this first stoneware is generic. There seem to be no distinguishing marks on the ware, and it is doubtful that any could be indentified.

Advertising flier, early 1920s.

On August 19, 1926, George Brush presented the design of an acorn to the board of directors for use as a trademark and a stamped mark on the stoneware. The board recommended that a patent attorney be consulted and if the acorn mark was not already taken, that it be adopted. Trademarks are submitted to the Patent and Design Office for a trial period, during which the design can be challenged by the industry. We have found no record that the design was ever formally submitted to the Patent and Design Office.

The 1929 Brush Pottery catalog showed several pieces of stoneware with the acorn mark. Brush acted as the sole distributor of Watt ware from 1926 until 1931. During this period of time the Brush Pottery was the majority share-owner of Watt Pottery capital stock.

The 1929 Brush Pottery catalog featuring Watt produced stoneware with the acorn mark.

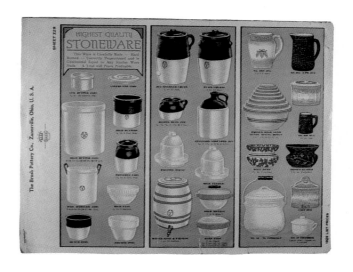

Apparently, the acorn was too similar to the existing mark of another pottery. The Uhl Pottery used an acorn but it is much more ornate than the one used by Watt. The Cambridge Art Pottery, in nearby Cambridge, Ohio used a simpler acorn mark that is closer in style to the Watt acorn. In the early 1930s, the acorn was replaced with an eagle as the mark on the stoneware.

The 1933 Brush Pottery catalog features the Watt eagle on one piece of stoneware. It is interesting to note that 1933 is two years after Brush relinquished control of the Watt Pottery, although George Brush was still sales manager of the Watt Pottery and the Brush Pottery was still selling at least some of the Watt Pottery's output.

The eagle mark was stamped in blue cobalt on the ware, with the gallonage marked in the center. The eagle mark became the corporate emblem of the Watt Pottery, in use throughout the remainder of the pottery's history.

The Watt Pottery abruptly curtailed production of stoneware in 1935, probably because of falling sales revenues, and introduced the early kitchen and oven ware.

EARLY KITCHEN AND OVEN WARE, 1935 - mid-1940s

The very earliest products of this era are not well identified. Only a few photographs of ware from this period, from W.I. Watt's archives, are available. They show banded mixing bowls similar in style to the Bak-Ezee line of 1940. It is not known if the patterns from the mid 1930s were marked.

The 1933 Brush Pottery catalog. The Watt eagle appears on the butter jar.

The authors have not located any of these unusual tree bark jardinieres. They were produced in the 1930s.

By the late 1930s, The Watt Pottery began marking the bottom of the ware. The words "Oven Ware - Made In U.S.A." were marked in the mold on most pieces. Some ware from this time period bears only the size of the bowl, not the full mark. The authors have not located "Oven Ware" as a registered trademark, but it appears on nearly all pieces of Watt ware from the late 1930s until the end of production in 1965.

Most patterns from this period were known by a numbering system instead of by name. Series numbers that the authors have found in production records are: 43, 140, 142, 145, 146, 150, 155 and 156. Boxed sets of ware may be found which have one of these numbers stamped on them. Only two series numbers have been matched with patterns, 145 and 146. These two patterns have been named "Arcs" and "Loops" by the authors. Other names for patterns from this era are "Moon & Stars", "Raised Button" and "Diamonds", all simply named from their appearance. Bak-Ezee, decorated with blue and white bands, is the only early kitchen and oven ware which is marked in the mold with a Watt trade name.

The shapes of all the ware from this period are very similar in nature, with all patterns sharing only a few different mold shapes. There are mixing bowls, covered casseroles, pie plates, individual lug-handled casseroles, and pitchers and canisters. The most common color is a tan, or salmon color, with blue and green the next most common glaze colors. Yellow and pink are found on a few pieces.

The shape of the bowls and casseroles is the main distinguishing characteristic of ware from this period. They feature a heavy upper shoulder which is unglazed on the top and bottom edges. This enabled the ware to be stacked in the kiln without the pieces firing together. Lids also have unglazed areas on the top of the knob and directly underneath on the inside of the lid and can be stacked also. Early kitchen and oven ware was fired in periodic kilns in which the pieces had to be stacked.

We do not know the exact date production of this ware ended. During the transition period of the 1940s, the Watt Pottery produced several patterns which still used the "Oven Ware - Made In U.S.A." mark.

A Watt catalog page showing pattern No. 145 (Arcs) and No. 146 (Loops). The "modern bean pot" is pictured in Chapter 4.

Early kitchen and oven ware bowls are stacked seventy deep. There are over 10,000 bowls in this small corner of the warehouse.

TRANSITION WARE, 1949-1953

The authors have categorized the ware produced from about 1943 until 1950 as "Transition Ware". The shape of the ware changed from the old-fashioned look of the early kitchen and oven ware, to pieces which resembled the hand-decorated ware of the 1950s, but without the hand-decorated patterns. The Watt Pottery also began the production of embossed ware glazed in solid colors with designs embossed on the outside of the ware.

The bottom marks also went through a transition during this period. Several patterns from this era, such as Kla-Ham'rd, Swirl and Embossed Wreath, still used the "Oven Ware - Made in U.S.A." mark. But on other pieces the mark was shortened to the familiar "Oven Ware U.S.A." that would appear on Watt ware from then on.

One of the most picturesque of the Watt bottom marks is from the late 1940s, the Eve-N-Bake mark. This mark features the large "W" in a circular field, and is basically the Watt corporate emblem minus the eagle. (See Chapter 32 for bottom marks.) The Eve-N-Bake pieces were the basis for many of the molds which were hand-decorated in the Classic patterns.

CLASSIC PATTERNS

In late 1948 the Watt Pottery took a major step and hired the first decorators to begin work on the hand-decorated pottery which is so sought after today. By the summer of 1949, the first pattern, Rio Rose, was in production.

A remarkably small number of female decorators produced a tremendous quantity of ware. The decorators had mere sec-

onds to complete each piece. Five sets of tables each held three decorators. Three of the tables were supplied by the three conveyor belt systems in the pottery. The other tables were supplied from huge, multi-tiered carts filled with ware. As ware streamed down the conveyor, the first decorator at each table picked up a piece and deftly painted the main pattern, such as an apple or flower. She set the piece aside and the next decorator added leaves or stems. The third decorator completed the piece, adding the final parts of the design.

Each woman held the piece just long enough to paint it with a few brush strokes. Usually, a decorator only applied one color of glaze, to eliminate changing brushes. Those who painted two colors, or needed different brush widths, held several brushes at once between their fingers. The thin bands of color around the outside of the ware were applied using a hand-spun turntable. Each bowl was set onto an arbor on a vertical shaft. As the arbor was spun by hand, the women painted the bowls by holding a brush to the spinning bowl with their other hand.

Although several of the Watt decorators had some formal artistic training, most learned to decorate by trying. New employees were shown how to hold the brushes, how much glaze to apply, and how to twist their wrist to produce the simple shapes of the Watt patterns. Several recalled that they would borrow brushes and ware at first to practice at home. Others practiced with brushes and pieces of cardboard instead of pottery. Soon, each was skilled enough to take a regular place at one of the tables.

Watt decorators at work in 1949. The conveyor belt is in the rear in this photograph. These are small tables with one or two decorators at each one. Note the small turntables on the left tables, used to spin each piece while the colored bands are brushed on the outside of hand-decorated ware.

Three decorators work together towards the back of this scene. The woman on the far left is removing dried ware from the conveyor belt. The woman in the foreground is dipping ware in the final glaze and placing it on the conveyor to the kiln. In the original photograph it can be seen that these are Swirl bowls being dipped. The decorators are working on Rio Rose bowls in the background.

The decorators have fond memories of working for the Watts. Harry and Thomas Watt would often walk among the tables to observe production. Occasionally, one would have a comment on the decorating, but it was always in the form of a suggestion, not a demand. One decorator recalled that one day Harry Watt asked her to make her tulips larger. A while later, Thomas Watt spotted the large tulips and asked her if she could make them smaller. Her solution... when either of the Watt brothers walked by, she would make the tulips larger or smaller to suit his preference!

Until 1949, the Watt Pottery had seldom advertised their ware in periodical publications. Advertisements for Watt-produced ware were placed by the distributors of the ware, such as the George Borgfelt Corp.[1] But in December, 1949, the pottery began a regular ad campaign in the trade journals that would last throughout the 1950s and into the 1960s. The first advertisements were for the Tropical and Moonflower patterns, introduced at the Pittsburg Pottery and Glass Exhibit held in January, 1950. Month after month, the new Watt ware was featured in advertisements and new product articles.

The Watt Pottery's display at the historic 1950 Pittsburg Glass and Pottery Exhibit, when their first hand-decorated ware was introduced to the public. W.I. Watt is on the left. Behind Mr. Watt is Rio Rose ware. The ware on the table is Moonflower. To the right rear are pieces of Dogwood and Tropical.

Patterns from the classic pattern period are: Rio Rose (several variations), "Cross-Hatch Pansy", Dogwood, Daisy, Moonflower (two colors), Tropical and the original Starflower. The majority of ware from this period features the script Watt bottom mark. Some ware, particularly Rio Rose, can be found with an "R F Spaghetti" mark or a later "Oven Ware U.S.A." mark. (See Chapter 32 for bottom marks.)

Most of the molds for the ware made during this period are similar to the Eve-N-Bake shapes from the late 1940s, but the embossed ridges have been removed from around the bottom of the bowls and from around the lids. These shapes feature a heavy, rounded lip, or a lip and shoulder combination, around the outer rim of the pieces. Casseroles have a recessed area formed in the bowl into which the lid fits. This style of casserole was replaced with more modern designs by the mid-1950s.

A distinguishing characteristic of the classic hand-decorated patterns is that the designs are more complex than the modern patterns' designs. Most leaves feature veins which were incised (Rio Rose, original Starflower), or painted (Tropical, Moonflower, Dogwood). More colors and brush strokes were used than in the modern patterns. The number of brush strokes may vary with the size of the piece. The following chart lists the colors and the number of brush strokes for the larger pieces.

PATTERN	COLORS	BRUSH STROKES
Tropical	4	53 + painted veins
Daisy	5	28
Dogwood	3	27 + painted veins
Cross-Hatch Pansy	3	14
Rio Rose (Bullseye)	3	33 + incised veins
Rio Rose (early)	4	11 + incised veins
Rio Rose (later, plain leaf)	4	11
Starflower	3	24 + incised veins

MODERN PATTERNS, 1952-1965

The modern pattern era began in 1952 when the Apple pattern was introduced. Starflower underwent its first pattern reduction at this time. Original Starflower had six petals on the flower and incised veins on the leaves. By 1952 the pattern called 5-petal Starflower was advertised, with one less petal and no incised veins on the leaves.

In all probability, the switch to modern patterns was for economic reasons. Ware needed to be decorated very quickly in order to be sold in the low price market. The veins on the leaves took time to do, and led to quality problems with rough edges. The painted veins solved the roughness problem, but still took time. Using more glaze colors and brush strokes led to longer decorating time and higher production cost. The modern patterns were remarkably economical to produce. A large, hand-decorated piece could be sold for only about $.08 more than a banded piece in the later years of production.

Compare the following list of selected modern patterns with the list in the previous section:

PATTERN	COLORS	BRUSH STROKES
5-petal Starflower	2	13
4-petal Starflower	2	8
3-leaf Apple	3	10
2-leaf Apple	2	6
Reduced Apple	2	3
Autumn Foliage	1	11
Tulip	3	9
Dutch Tulip	3	18
Rooster	3	33 (approx.)

Note the small number of brush strokes required for some of the patterns: Apple (6 or 10 strokes), 4-petal Starflower (8 strokes), Autumn Foliage (11 strokes). The Reduced Apple pattern is very efficient in that it only required three brush strokes to produce a credible apple and leaves. The Rooster and Dutch Tulip patterns required the most brush strokes. Pieces in these patterns are among the hardest to find today. The wholesale price for a Rooster piece was about 5% more than the same piece in Apple. This higher cost may be one reason that the production life of Rooster and Dutch Tulip was fairly short.

Several of the Watt hand-decorated patterns have one or more simplifications of the pattern which were referred to by W.I. Watt as "reductions." These consist of fewer brush strokes, fewer glaze colors, and the elimination of certain elements of the design.

The first hand-decorated pattern, Rio Rose, has several variations, some of which seem to be sequential. The earliest photographs of Rio Rose (from 1949), all show the pattern called Bullseye by today's collectors. This is a relatively "busy" pattern, with concentric rings of red and green glaze. All pieces of Bullseye also feature incised veins in the leaves, and many have additional zig-zag, or "S"-shaped design elements.

The reduced Rio Rose pattern has incised veins in the leaves (often called "cut-leaf" by collectors), but no bullseye rings. Both versions of Rio Rose are shown in the 1952 Watt catalog. This reduced pattern may not have replaced Bullseye, but may have been offered as a simpler alternative. The version of Rio Rose found on pieces attributed to a later period, is the plain-leaf version. This reduction eliminates the incised veins in the leaves, and would appear to have replaced the earlier versions.

One pattern reduction familiar to collectors is the 2-leaf Apple pattern (as compared to 3-leaf). In this case, it is not possible to date Apple pieces by the number of leaves. 3-leaf Apple was featured in the catalogs and advertisements from the beginning of Apple production in 1952 until the pottery's end in 1965. 2-leaf Apple was probably offered to chain stores as a lower-cost alternative to 3-leaf Apple. The most dramatically reduced Apple pattern is Reduced Apple. It was a limited production variation made for an unknown customer.

Starflower does appear to have undergone sequential pattern reductions. Original Starflower, introduced in 1951, had six leaves and incised veins. By 1952, 5-petal Starflower was advertised. Starflower was further reduced to four petals with no bud around 1959, judging by the molds that each pattern is found on.

Other pieces of Watt ware were not hand-decorated. Ware with bands of colored glaze made up a significant portion of the pottery's production. All banded ware features three heavy bands of colored slip. Some have all bands of one color, while others use bands of two contrasting colors. Band widths and spacing vary with the size and shape of each piece.

Banded ware was decorated very rapidly using a simple device. For each combination of band width and spacing, a copper container was fabricated which held about a gallon of slip. Tubing emerged from the bottom of the container, and each tube ended in a nozzle of the proper width. Out of the top of the container was a tube with a mouth piece.

The bander worked at a bench with a spinning shaft which had an arbor on the end. The container of prepared slip was placed on a pivoting wooden shelf and adjusted so that the nozzles were pointed at the proper height. The bander grabbed a bowl, quickly placed it over the spinning arbor and held it in place with nothing more than the end of his finger while the bowl whirled away. Placing his lips on the mouth piece, he gently blew into the tube and forced three streams of slip to spray onto the bowl. Properly done, each bowl now had thick colored bands around it. These bands can easily be distinguished from the thin bands painted on by the decorators.

This operation required a great deal of skill and coordination. Although today we recognize the hand-decorators as skilled artisans, the bander was actually the highest paid worker in the decorating and glazing department. This was probably due to the high output of the bander, as a result of the semi-automated nature of the work.

The bander at work.

Watt also made some ware which was stencil-decorated using sprayed slip to produce the pattern. The Eagle was the only actual pattern which was done using this technique. The words on "Goodies" jars and the "Corn", "Nuts", "Pretzels", "Chips" snack set were stenciled onto the ware. Lids for the "Flour", "Sugar", "Coffee" and "Tea" canisters had the words stamped, like the advertising pieces.

The Orchard Ware patterns used two more methods of decorating. For the dripped glazes, the ware was given a base coat of glaze, and when it had sufficiently dried, the piece was placed upside-down over a "U"-shaped rod, and the top of the piece was dipped into a contrasting color glaze. After the piece was turned over, the contrasting glaze ran unevenly down the sides. There are many different color combinations of drip ware. The other method of decorating Orchard Ware was to sprinkle the glazed ware with small specks of contrasting powdered glaze.

Throughout the 1950s, the shape of the Watt bowls underwent changes to become more modern. In 1950, the Classic pattern bowls all had lips, or lips and shoulders around the rim. Casserole lids fit into a recess in the bowl. In 1953, the 50 series of bakers (#52, #53, #54, #55) was introduced. These were a simpler shape, with no rim, but still retained the deeply curved profile of the classic pattern ware. Lids were a flattened dome shape, similar to the earlier lids, but rested on top of the bowl, not in a recess. This enabled a bowl to be sold as an open or a covered baker with no change in the mold.

In 1955, the 60 series began production (#60, #66, #67, #68). These bowls have a clean, slightly curved, profile in keeping with the more modern look. The lids had become a simple dome shape with a less-pronounced edge.

In 1959, the Orchard Ware series, molds #106 through #132, was introduced. Most of these pieces were designed by Eva Zeisel (see next section).

In 1962, the ribbed 600 series bowls replaced the #04 through #07 nappies and the traditional 5" through 9" mixing bowls were replaced with a ribbed design. Lids on the #600 and #601 covered bakers compliment the funnel lids of the Orchard Ware bowls.

THE INFLUENCE OF EVA ZEISEL

In late 1954, an unlikely meeting of modern art and the country-styled Watt ware occurred when famed designer Eva Zeisel was commissioned to produce a line of ware for the Watt Pottery.

Eva Polanyi Stricker was born in Budapest, Hungary in 1906, to a fairy wealthy family. At the age of seventeen, she entered the Royal Academy of Fine Arts to study painting. After only three semesters, however, she withdrew and decided to learn a craft instead. At the suggestion of her mother, Eva became apprenticed to a local potter.

Her six-month apprenticeship taught her the basics of preparing clay, throwing, glazing and firing the ware. She mixed clay with her bare feet and did all the odd jobs expected of any apprentice. At the age of eighteen and a half, she started her own pottery. After only a year of designing her own ware, the Hungarian government sent some of her pieces to their display in the 1926 Philadelphia Sesquicentennial in America, where the young woman's pottery received an honorable mention.

A pottery in Budapest created an art department and hired Eva to design vases and tea sets. When the pottery returned to producing sanitary ware the following year, Eva began a series of jobs for potteries which reformed her focus from handicraft to industrial design. During this period she designed a wide range of different ware. By 1932 she had become one of many foreign designers working in the Soviet Union. In 1934 she began designing for the Dulevo factory near Moscow. There she was given the task of creating a set of standardized dinnerware to be used throughout the Soviet Union. Her design was short-lived, as the government soon abolished the concept of standardization.

In 1937, most foreigners in the Soviet Union were removed from their positions. After a short refuge in Vienna, she left Austria on the only train allowed across the border to Switzerland on the very day that German troops invaded Austria. In refuge in England, she married Hans Zeisel, whom she had met earlier. With law and order collapsing in Europe, the Zeisels came to America.

Establishing her own contacts through trade publications, Zeisel found work designing several sets of ceramic giftware. In 1939 she began teaching at the Pratt Institute in Brooklyn. Many

of her students went on to become successful designers. In 1942, Zeisel designed *Stratoware*, a streamlined dinnerware set for Sears, Roebuck and Co. The same year she designed *Utility Ware*. This set of dinnerware featured many concepts which she was to carry through to other lines, such as standarization of sizes to reduce the number of lids and molds.

Zeisel's major breakthrough was her commission to produce *Museum* dinnerware for the Castleton China Co. The Museum of Modern Art had recommended Zeisel to Castleton. This was the first modern-styled, American dinnerware designed for formal use. The acclaim which Zeisel received from *Museum* drew the attention of the president of the Red Wing Pottery in Minnesota. Her Red Wing dinnerware, *Town and Country*, features whimsical, fluid shapes which were radical departures from conventional American dinnerware. The shapes of her *Town and Country* salt and pepper shakers were mirrored in the cartoon characters the "Shmoos", drawn by Al Capp.

During the next decade, Zeisel designed wares for many companies, such as Sears, Roebuck and Co., Western Stoneware, Charm House, Riverside Ceramic Co., and General Mills. She designed perfume bottles for Charles of the Ritz and a line of modern furniture. Around 1950, she designed her most popular dinnerware, *Hallcraft/Tomorrow's Classic*, for the Hall China Co. of East Liverpool, Ohio. In 1953 she was appointed artistic director for the A.T. Heisey glass company. She also designed glassware for the Federal Glass Co.

Zeisel has forgotten the exact details of her acquaintance with W.I. Watt, but during one of his many trips to New York City, the two met and a line of pottery was commissioned on a trial basis. Zeisel was given an unused room at the Watt Pottery for her use in designing the dinnerware. Mr. Watt left her in complete creative control of the shapes and decoration.

Zeisel designed a series of 18 pieces, which Mr. Watt numbered from 101 through 118. The design combines the simple, country look of Watt ware with elements of the Modernism movement. She named the pieces, "South Mountain Stoneware", after her new home on South Mountain Road. It was the only ware she ever marked this way. To Mr. Watt, the most controversial aspect of the ware was the unusual decoration, a series of animal caricatures drawn in the Modernism style by a friend of Zeisel, French artist, Michel Cadoret. He called the animals the "Jungle Barnyard." The animals (shown in Chapter 29) were stamped in black slip on several different colored backgrounds: cream, ivory, and a beautiful almond glaze with fine brown specks. Only four display samples of each of the 18 shapes were produced according to Mr. Watt's records.[2]

South Mountain Stoneware was shown at the 1955 Pittsburg Glass and Pottery Exhibit, but the radical look of the dinnerware did not generate sufficient orders from purchasers. Mr. Watt elected not to produce the line.

While researching this story, the authors had assumed that none of this ware ever saw production. Upon examining Zeisel's archived samples, however, a remarkable realization was made - nearly all of her shapes were produced! Eva Zeisel's South Mountain Stoneware, without the Jungle Barnyard animals, was the basis for the Orchard Ware series of shapes.

The elements of Zeisel's designs which are the most familiar to collectors of Watt ware are the hourglass shapes of the #115 coffee carafe and the #117 and #118 salt and pepper shakers, the recurved #106 salad bowl, the "funnel" lids on the #01 grease jar and #110 casserole, and the #112 tea pot.

Zeisel's original #115 carafe had no handle or spout. W.I. Watt added handles in two different styles for production. Zeisel's #112 tea pot featured a rattan, bail handle. Mr. Watt changed this to a conventional pitcher handle. Her #110 casserole and its funnel lid are unchanged, and so are the hourglass salt and pepper shakers.

Comparison of the three different shapes for the #115. In the center is a carafe in Bronze Luster with no handle or spout. This is the original Zeisel design for this piece. On the left is the covered coffee server with pitcher-style handle. On the right is the carafe with ribbon handle, we do not believe this style ever came with a lid.

Evolution of the Watt tea pot shape. On the left is a Zeisel #112 in white glaze, with lugs for the bail handle (handle and lids removed for comparison). On the right is a production #112. Watt changed the handle to a style more suited to match the rest of the line.

Mr. Watt did not use her sugar and creamer design. The 1/2 pint #62 pitcher, matching the other Watt pitchers, became a creamer. A sugar bowl, with a flared top similar in profile to Zeisel's mug, was designed. True to Zeisel's design economies, the Watt sugar bowl shares a common lid with the tea pot, just as South Mountain Stoneware did. Also in keeping with her principles, the lid from the #110 fits the #130 and #131 bowls which Mr. Watt added, and was also used to cover the existing #96 baker. Zeisel's mug and coffee cup designs were not used. (The shape of the coffee cup is unknown at this time.)

Mr. Watt added the molds #119 through #133 to the line. The #130 and #131 casseroles share the lid with the #110, and the #126 cruets adopt the hourglass shape of Zeisel's shakers. This line of ware, marked "Orchard Ware" on the bottom, was probably first marketed through the firm of Newland, Schneeloch and Piek, who have the Orchard Ware name registered. The Orchard Ware shapes are the most modern of all the Watt pieces. Most were introduced in 1959, four years after Eva Zeisel designed them.

ADVERTISING PREMIUM WARE

One of the endearing traits of Watt pottery is that it was often given away as premiums. It was inexpensive, but colorfully decorated and cheerful. Other dinnerware was produced as premium ware also, the most familiar being depression glass. Some of the Watt premium ware was simply standard ware given away or made available with purchases of certain items or services. But, much of the Watt ware has a feature which sets it apart from other companies' premium ware - advertising. Boldly stamped on the front of the ware, it is a feature which seems to have been used by few other dinnerware producers. Throughout the 1950s, the Watt Pottery was listed in the *Crockery and Glass Journal* annual directories as a supplier of premium ware. Other producers of premium ware were listed, but we must bear in mind the difference between premium ware and *advertising* premium ware.

Advertising premium ware from Christmas, 1957.

The advertising was imprinted onto the dried and decorated ware before the piece was dipped into the final, clear glaze. To accomplish this, each separate advertising slogan had to have a custom rubber stamp made. All of the stamps used by the Watt Pottery were made by one company, the Hiss Stamp Company.

Located in nearby Columbus, Ohio, the Hiss Stamp Company has been in business since 1889.

Each rubber stamp was made from a zinc engraving, an old method made obsolete by today's new technology. The zinc masters were stored for many years to enable reorders, but our contact at Hiss Stamp informed us that the masters for the Watt account were thrown out years ago.

Advertising was offered to customers on the full range of Watt ware. The Watt records for laying out the advertising contain charts of imprints for all common pieces except the tea pots. The cost for advertising varied with the size of the imprint and the amount of ware ordered, but was about three cents per piece. Customers also had to pay for the zinc masters to produce the rubber stamps.

To demonstrate the advertising, a kit of advertising salesman samples was available (see catalog reprint section). The sample kit was for sale, indicating that it could be purchased and used by other sales organizations besides the Watt Pottery's. Salesman's samples can be identified by the imprint on them. They are marked with statements such as: "This is an imprint for this size bowl." Larger pieces have a more extensive imprint.

The imprint on a typical advertising salesman sample.

Each of these 600 series Apple bowls is an advertising salesman sample. The imprint is progressively larger on each piece.

As mentioned, Watt ware with imprinted advertising could be sold by distributors of Watt ware, not just by Watt salesman. One such distributor was the Newton Manufacturing Company of Newton, Iowa. They took orders from their customers for a line of Watt advertising ware. Newton placed the order through the Watt Pottery, adding a markup for their profit. Watt then ordered the stamps from Hiss Stamp, produced the ware and shipped the order directly to Newton's customer.

An advertising salesman sample from the Newton Manufacturing Company. The part number, #33A, is a Watt Pottery pattern code for an Apple pie plate.

Watt advertising was imprinted using distinct, outlined letters. Most advertising was printed using black slip to color the letters, but a few customers specified red lettering. Advertising is most commonly found on the Apple, Cherry, Starflower, Autumn Foliage, and Kitch-N-Queen patterns, although some Rooster and Dutch Tulip pieces were imprinted. Tulip may have been sold exclusively through Woolworth stores and was probably not imprinted. Other colors of banded ware were imprinted, as was plain, clear-glazed ware with no pattern.

Most advertising premium ware was ordered by small businesses such as groceries, dairies, furniture stores and even the local banks. With the exception of ware made for the oil companies, very few pieces were made with national brand names imprinted. Occasionally a piece can be found with a company's logo in addition to the lettering.

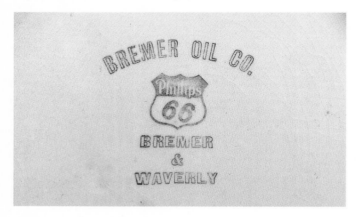

This advertising imprint features the Phillips 66 company logo. Most national brands mentioned on Watt ware are oil companies.

The only commemorative pieces known to the authors are for the "Pennsylvania Dutch Days" held in Hershey, Pennsylvania. Most of these pieces are imprinted on the Rooster pattern (why not Dutch Tulip?), but at least one year #75 bean cups with a cream upper half and a blue bottom were imprinted for the event. A surprisingly large number of pieces are found with messages placed by individuals or couples, usually to note a marriage or anniversary. Dated pieces, or pieces with early phone numbers are prized by many collectors. The earliest dated piece we have seen is from 1954.

TIME-LINE OF PATTERNS AND TRADE NAMES

This chart shows the earliest known date for the various Watt patterns and trade names. These dates are verified from advertisements, catalogs, and production records. If a name is listed here as "introduced", the authors have found a new product announcement. If a name is listed as "advertised", it is offered for sale at that time, but the introduction date is not known. If the name is shown as "listed", it has been found listed in a directory issue of a trade journal such as *The Crockery and Glass Journal*. As a general rule, the Watt Pottery only listed their patterns after they were in production. Names shown in all-capital letters are official names.

August, 1926	Acorn stoneware introduced.
1933	Eagle stoneware advertised.
1940	BAK-EZEE in production.
	Arcs and Loops patterns advertised.
June, 1943	Embossed wreath pattern advertised.
1944	GALA-COLOR pattern name listed.
	CABINART trade name listed.
	KLA-HAM'RD pattern name listed.
1948	GOLD-N-BAKE trade name listed.
June, 1949	RIO ROSE introduced.
	SWIRL in production.
January, 1950	TROPICAL introduced.
	MOONFLOWER introduced.
	DOGWOOD advertised.
1950	WILD ROSE pattern name listed.
	PAST-L pattern name listed.
January, 1951	STARFLOWER introduced.
January, 1952	RED APPLE introduced.
	Corn Row advertised.
	5-PETAL STARFLOWER advertised.
January, 1953	SILHOUETTE introduced.
	BLACK BEAUTY introduced (Orchard Ware glaze).
	GREENBRIAR introduced (Orchard Ware glaze).
January, 1954	KOLOR-KRAFT introduced.
January, 1955	ROOSTER introduced.
	JUNGLE BARNYARD introduced.
	KITCH-N-QUEEN introduced.
January, 1956	PENNSYLVANIA DUTCH introduced (Dutch Tulip).
1957	AMERICAN RED BUD advertised.

1958	MORNING-GLORY advertised.		WESTWOOD introduced (Orchard Ware glaze).
	Owens WOOD GRAIN introduced.	1962	BROWN-STONE advertised.
			TULIP advertised.
January, 1959	AUTUMN Foliage introduced.	1963	WOOD GRAIN advertised.
January, 1960	PAR-T-QUE introduced (3 brown bands).		

Watt Ware

PATENT OFFICE

FEB 12 1952

DESIGN DIVISION

**CATALOG
REPRINTS**

21-A   19-A   42-A   43-A   40-A 41-A

18-S   17-S   16-S   15-S

FA   20-D   EB

39-W

31-W   25-D

1952 catalog cover.

Beautiful — "Under Glaze" Hand Painted Permanent Decoration • *Each piece is ovenware pottery* • Lovely, heat resistant, Party, Barbeque, and Casual Service • Informal Table Service • Picnics • Kitchen and Ovenware, for Every Use

THE WATT POTTERY COMPANY
CROOKSVILLE, OHIO

1958 catalog cover.

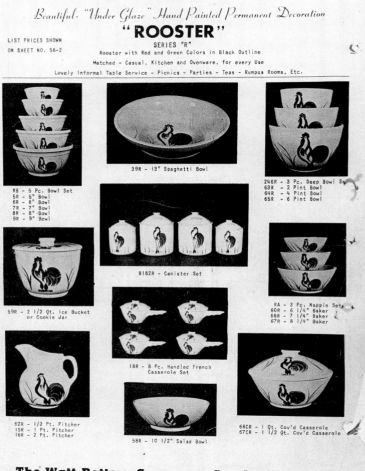

1956 catalog.

NO. 200 SALESMAN KIT ADVERTISING SPECIALTY ITEMS

This kit is an excellent way for your salesman to show customers the various items that can be *imprinted*, in three different patterns. The pitcher shows Ad Copy on outside collar, the mixing bowls, and Covered Casseroles will have Ad Copy on inside bottom.

The kit measures 23 ¼" long, 9 ¼" wide, 7 ¼" deep, in a beautiful maroon color box. These are available with sample piece at a minimum cost.

$4.95 each Net. F.O.B. FACTORY

MIXING BOWLS   PITCHERS

1958 catalog.

"RED APPLE"

LIST PRICES SHOWN
ON SHEET NO. 58-1

SERIES "A"
Apple with Green Stem and Two Tone Green Leaves

Matched — Casual, Kitchen and Ovenware, for Every Use

Lovely Informal Table Service • Picnics • Parties • Teas • Rumpus Rooms, Etc.

8182A — Canister Set

246A — 3 Pc— Deep Bowl Set
63A — 2 Pt. Bowl
64A — 4 Pt. Bowl
65A — 6 Pt. Bowl

AB — 5 Pc. Bowl Set
5A — 5" Mixing Bowl
6A — 6" Mixing Bowl
7A — 7" Mixing Bowl
8A — 8" Mixing Bowl
9A — 9" Mixing Bowl

0A — 4 Piece Nappy Set
See Price List Bulk Pack

62A — 1/2 Pt. Pitcher
15A — 1 Pt. Pitcher
16A — 2 Pt. Pitcher
17A — 4 Pt. Pitcher

59A — 2 1/2 Qt. Ice Bucket
and Cookie Jar

92A — Cookie Jar and Cover

AA — 3 Pc. Nappie Set
60A — 6 1/4" Open Baker
66A — 7 1/4" Open Baker
67A — 8 1/4" Open Baker

66CA — 1 Qt. Cov'd. Casserole
67CA — 1 1/2 Qt. Cov'd. Casserole

73A — 9¾" Salad

1958 catalog.

LATTICE - MORNING GLORY

SERIES "MC"

LIST PRICES SHOWN
ON SHEET NO. 58-2

HIGHLY EMBOSSED LATTICE AND MORNING GLORY PATTERN WITH

BRILLIANT RED AND GREEN UNDER GLAZE COLORS

Matched - Casual, Kitchen and Ovenware, for every Use
Lovely Informal Table Service - Picnics - Parties - Teas - Rumpus Rooms. Etc.

C94MC - 2 QUART CASSEROLE AND COVER

95MC - COOKIE JAR AND COVER

MCB 5 PIECE BOWL SET
5MC - 5" Embossed Bowl
6MC - 6" Embossed Bowl
7MC - 7" Embossed Bowl
8MC - 8" Embossed Bowl
9MC - 9" Embossed Bowl

978MC - CREAMER AND SUGAR

96MC - 4 PINT PITCHER
97MC - 1/2 PINT PITCHER

94MC - 8 1/2" OPEN BAKER

LIST PRICES SHOWN ON SHEET No. 58-4

"KITCH-N-QUEEN" Pink and Turquoise Band Ovenware

SERIES "F"

For Food Preparing, Fine Oven Cooking and Food Storing

"Matched" Design Kitchen Pottery made of yellow American stoneware clay with High Gloss finish makes a fine line of ware for full flavored tasty cooking and valued home use.

66CF — 1-Quart Covered Casserole
67CF — 1½-Quart Covered Casserole

246F — 3-Pc. Bowl Set
63F — Bowl; 2-Pint
64F — Bowl; 4-Pint
65F — Bowl; 6-Pint

FB — 5 Pc. Bowl Set
5F — 5" Mixing Bowl
6F — 6" Mixing Bowl
7F — 7" Mixing Bowl
8F — 8" Mixing Bowl
9F — 9" Mixing Bowl

FA — 3-Pc. Nappie (Baker) Set
60F — 6¼" Open Baker
66F — 7¼" Open Baker
67F — 8¼" Open Baker

59F — 2½-Quart Ice Bucket
or Cookie Jar

10F — 10" Mixing Bowl
12F — 12" Mixing Bowl
14F — 14" Mixing Bowl
616F — 16" Mixing Bowl

1958 catalog.

1958 catalog.

1959 catalog cover.

Watt Ware For 1959

98V	62V	VB	AV
OA	02A	110A	304 JARDINIERE
76	5	7	
17F	59F	FB	

Beautiful — "Under Glaze" Hand Painted Permanent Decoration • Each piece is ovenware pottery • Lovely, heat resistant, Party, Barbecue, and Casual Service • Informal Table Service • Picnics • Kitchen and Ovenware, for Every Use

THE WATT POTTERY COMPANY
CROOKSVILLE, OHIO

LIST PRICES SHOWN ON SHEET No. 58-5

"WATT WARE" Oven and Kitchenware Items

All Ovenware ... Specialty Pieces ... Practical and Useful

6" Dog Dish
7" Dog Dish

JARDINIERES
No. 300 — 4½" Yellow Jardiniere
No. 301 — 5½" White Jardiniere
No. 302 — 6½" Pink Jardiniere
No. 303 — 7½" Green Jardiniere
No. 304 — 8¾" White Jardiniere

EB — 5 Piece Bowl Set
5E — 5" Yellow Bowl
6E — 6" Pink Bowl
7E — 7" Turquoise Bowl
8E — 8" White Bowl
9E — 9" Green Bowl

No. 7374 — 9 Piece Salad Set — Green

No. 756 — 8 Pc Bean Pot Set
No. 75 — 8 ounce Individual Open Bean Pots

No. 71 BIRD BATH
Stone Finish - White

1958 catalog

LIST PRICES SHOWN IN SHEET No. 59-1

"KITCH-N-QUEEN" Pink and Turquoise Band Ovenware
SERIES "F"

For Food Preparing, Fine Oven Cooking and Food Storing

"Matched" Design Kitchen Pottery made of yellow American stoneware clay with High Gloss finish makes a fine line of ware for full flavored tasty cooking and valued home use.

FB—5 Pc. Bowl Set
5F—5" Mixing Bowl
6F—6" Mixing Bowl
7F—7" Mixing Bowl
8F—8" Mixing Bowl
9F—9" Mixing Bowl

110F—2 Qt. Casserole and Cover

246F—3-Pc. Bowl Set
63F—Bowl; 2-Pint
64F—Bowl; 4-Pint
65F—Bowl; 6-Pint

17F—5 Pt. Pitcher w/ Ice Guard

0F—4 Pc. Nappy Set
04F—6½ Oz. Nappy
05F—14½ Oz. Nappy
06F—25½ Oz. Nappy
07F—48½ Oz. Nappy

59F—2½-Quart Ice Bucket or Cookie Jar

10F—10" Mixing Bowl
12F—12" Mixing Bowl
14F—14" Mixing Bowl
616F—16" Mixing Bowl

1959 catalog.

Beautiful "Under Glaze" Hand Painted Permanent Decoration
"RED APPLE"
SERIES "A"

Apple with Green Stem and Two Tone Green Leaves
Matched—Casual, Kitchen and Ovenware, for Every Use.
Lovely Informal Table Service — Picnics — Parties — Teas — Rumpus Rooms, Etc.

AB—5-Pc. Bowl Set
5A—5" Mixing Bowl
6A—6" Mixing Bowl
7A—7" Mixing Bowl
8A—8" Mixing Bowl
9A—9" Mixing Bowl

76A—Cookie Jar or Bean Pot

246A—3-Pc. Deep Bowl Set
63A—2 Pt. Bowl
64A—4 Pt. Bowl
65A—6 Pt. Bowl

73A—9¾" Salad

62A—½ Pt. Pitcher
15A—1 Pt. Pitcher
16A—2 Pt. Pitcher
17A—4 Pt. Pitcher w/Guard

96A—8¼" Open Baker

OA—4-Piece Nappy Set
See Price List Bulk Pack

505A—32 Ounce Tea Pot & Cover

112A—6 Cup Tea Pot And Cover

110A—2 Quart Casserole and Cover

121A—11 Ounce Mug

1959 catalog.

STONEWARE SPECIALTY ITEMS

All Pieces Fired to 2000 Degrees Fahrenheit. Will Stand Heat or Cold, and will
Retain These Temperatures Longer Than Ordinary Containers.

6" Dog Dish
7" Dog Dish
Brown and Green

76—2 Qt. Bean Pot and Cover
93—1½ Qt. Bean Pot and Cover
502—1 Gal. Bean Pot and Cover
Brown Only
See Price List For Sets

5" Kitty Dish
Turquoise and Yellow

75—8 oz. Open Individual Bean Pot
77—16 oz. Open Individual Bean Pot
Brown Only

No. 400 — 2 Gallon Iced Tea Dispenser
With Approved Faucet
Brown Color
For Trade Name See Price List.

No. 401 — 2 Gallon Lemonade Dispenser
With Approved Faucet
Lemon Color

Beautiful — "Under Glaze" Hand Painted Permanent Decoration • Each piece
is ovenware pottery • Lovely, heat resistant, Party, Barbecue, and Casual Service
• Informal Table Service • Picnics • Kitchen and Ovenware, for Every Use

FB — 110F — 1111 F—Range Set — 503F
110VS — 506V — 94V — 39V
1219A — 16A — 505A — 119A
S-302 — 6"-7" — 504 — 76 — SWB

1961 catalog cover.

1959 catalog.

"AUTUMN FOLIAGE"
SERIES "V"

Buff glaze with contrasting brown leaves on outside of every piece. Matched items which make excellent pieces for outdoor living. Also, used inside for kitchen, oven to table to refrigerator service.

9862V—Creamer and Sugar

503V—3 ½ Qt. Cookie Jar & Cover W/Handles

VB—5 Pc. Bowl Set
5V—5" Mixing Bowl
6V—6" Mixing Bowl
7V—7" Mixing Bowl
8V—8" Mixing Bowl
9V—9" Mixing Bowl

39V—13" Spaghetti Bowl

110VS—2 Quart Casserole And Cover W/Electric Heat Element In Ceramic Base

506V—24 Oz. Handled Casserole & Cover

62V—½ Pt. Pitcher
15V—1 Pt. Pitcher
16V—2 Pt. Pitcher
17V—4 Pt. Pitcher w/Guard

IIIIV—Range Set

94V—6 ¼" Salad or Soup Bowl

246V—3 Pc. Bowl Set
63V—2 Pt. Deep Bowl
64V—4 Pt. Deep Bowl
65V—6 Pt. Deep Bowl

THE WATT POTTERY COMPANY   CROOKSVILLE, OHIO

1961 catalog.

"KITCH-N-QUEEN"   Pink and Turquoise Band   Ovenware
SERIES "F"

For Food Preparing, Fine Oven Cooking and Food Storing

"Matched" Design Kitchen Pottery made of yellow American stoneware clay with High Gloss finish makes a fine line of ware for full flavored tasty cooking and valued home use.

10F—10" Mixing Bowl
12F—12" Mixing Bowl
14F—14" Mixing Bowl
616F—16" Mixing Bowl

246F—3-Pc. Bowl Set
63F—Bowl; 2-Pint
64F—Bowl; 4-Pint
65F—Bowl; 6-Pint

FB—5 Pc. Bowl Set
5F—5" Mixing Bowl
6F—6" Mixing Bowl
7F—7" Mixing Bowl
8F—8" Mixing Bowl
9F—9" Mixing Bowl

17F—5 Pt. Pitcher w/ Ice Guard
16F—2 Pt. Pitcher
15F—1 " "

1111F—4 Piece Range Set

73F—9 ¾" Salad Bowl

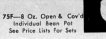

OF—4 Piece Nappy Set
O4F—6 ½ Oz. Nappy
O5F—14 ½ " "
O6F—25 ½ " "
O7F—48 ½ " "

503F—3 ½ Quart Cookie Jar & Cov. W/Handles

76F—2 Quart Bean Pot and Cover W/Handles

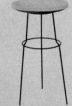

75F—8 Oz. Open & Cov'd Individual Bean Pot
See Price Lists For Sets

1961 catalog.

STONEWARE WITH ACCESSORIES

Here is a diversified line with metal components for Florist — Gifts — Outdoors and Living Room. The under glaze decoration is permanent, and each piece of these items are manufactured for longer-lasting life.

JARDINIERES WHITE and GREEN ASSORTED

S-302— 6 ½" Jardiniere Assorted w/Stand
S-303— 7 ½" Jardiniere Assorted w/Stand
S-304— 8 ¾" Jardiniere Assorted w/Stand
S-305—10 ½" Jardiniere Assorted w/Stand
S-306—13" Jardiniere Assorted w/Stand

10"—12"—14" Bowls are available on special order for Florists Pots in colors above.

71—Bird Bath White Only

Series "A" Apple or "V" Autumn Foliage

Under Glaze Decorated Items With Brass Accessories

1096A—1 ½ Qt. Casserole And Cover W/ Brass Stand and Warmer

119A—9" Salad Bowl W/Plastic Fork and Spoon And Brass Stand

1219A—Chip-N'-Dip W/Brass Stand And Dip Holder

1096V—1 ½ Qt. Casserole And Cover W/Brass Stand and Warmer

1219V—Chip N' Dip W/Brass Stand And Dip Holder

119V—9" Salad Bowl W/Plastic Fork and Spoon And Brass Stand

1961 catalog.

THE WATT POTTERY COMPANY   CROOKSVILLE, OHIO

LIST PRICES SHOWN
ON SHEET NO. 59-4

"RED APPLE"

SERIES "A"

Apple with Green Stem and Two Tone Green Leaves
Matched—Casual, Kitchen and Ovenware, for Every Use.
Lovely Informal Table Service — Picnics — Parties — Teas — Rumpus Rooms, Etc.

76A—Cookie Jar
or Bean Pot

246A—3-Pc. Deep Bowl Set
63A—2 Pt. Bowl
64A—4 Pt. Bowl
65A—6 Pt. Bowl

AB—5-Pc. Bowl Set
5A—5" Mixing Bowl
6A—6" Mixing Bowl
7A—7" Mixing Bowl
8A—8" Mixing Bowl
9A—9" Mixing Bowl

73A—9¾" Salad

62A—½ Pt. Pitcher
15A—1 Pt. Pitcher
16A—2 Pt. Pitcher
17A—4 Pt. Pitcher
w/Guard

02A—Pantry or
Refrigerator Set

OA—4-Piece Nappy Set
See Price List Bulk Pack

110A—2 Quart
Casserole and Cover

106A—11" Salad

117A—118A
Salt and Pepper

126A—Vinegar and Oil

18A—12 Oz. Individual
Lug Casserole
Open and Covered

1961 catalog.

Watt Ware For 1962

FB	601F	17F	503F
246B	1111B	73B	BN
39A	16A	600A	AN
306	6"-7"	504	76	EB

Beautiful — "Under Glaze" Hand Painted Permanent Decoration • Each piece
is ovenware pottery • Lovely, heat resistant, Party, Barbecue, and Casual Service
• Informal Table Service • Picnics • Kitchen and Ovenware, for Every Use

1962 catalog cover.

LIST PRICES SHOWN ON SHEET 61-5

STONEWARE SPECIALTY ITEMS

All Pieces Fired to 2000 Degrees Fahrenheit. Will Stand Heat or Cold, and will
Retain These Temperatures Longer Than Ordinary Containers.

504—6½" Spaniel
Dog Dish
Yellow, Copper and
Turquoise

5" Kitty Dish
Turquoise
and Yellow

6" Dog Dish
7" Dog Dish
Brown and Green

Cover For
No. 75 & 77
(Covers make it
possible to stack
the Pots. Also
used as Hot
Tile)

75—8 oz. Open & Cov'
Individual Bean Pot
77—16 oz. Open & Cov
Individual Bean Pot
Brown Only

76—2 Qt. Bean Pot
and Cover

93—1½ Qt. Bean Pot
and Cover

502—1 Gal. Bean Pot
and Cover
Above Brown Only
See Price List For Sets

YOUR
TRADE NAME
ICED TEA

No. 400-1—1 gallon
Tea Dispenser
No. 400-2—2 gallon
Tea Dispenser
No. 400-3—3 gallon
Tea Dispenser

Shown above with push-button
faucet. For Trade Name, see
Price List. No. 61-5.

Long-wearing, easy to clean
Wyott stainless steel faucets
with all the fine labor-saving
features; finger-tip control,
instant flow, no-drip automatic shut-off. Available with
all size tea dispensers at extra cost. See Price List No.
61-5.

SWB—5 Piece Bowls
5SW—5" Bowl-White
6SW—6"   Blue
7SW—7"   Yellow
8SW—8"   Green
9SW—9"   Copper

1961 catalog.

Watt Ware For 1963

WG 617W 608WC 613W

39A 16A 600A AN

FB 601F 17F 503F

6"-7" 504 76 No. 76G No. 59G No. 72G

Beautiful — "Under Glaze" Hand Painted Permanent Decoration • Each piece is ovenware pottery • Lovely, heat resistant, Party, Barbecue, and Casual Service • Informal Table Service • Picnics • Kitchen and Ovenware, for Every Use

THE WATT POTTERY COMPANY
CROOKSVILLE, OHIO

1963 catalog cover.

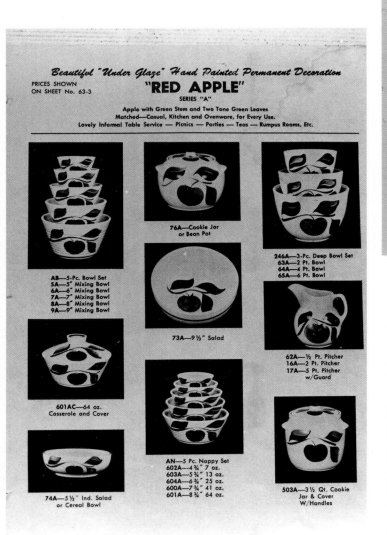

Beautiful "Under Glaze" Hand Painted Permanent Decoration
PRICES SHOWN ON SHEET No. 63-3
"RED APPLE"
SERIES "A"
Apple with Green Stem and Two Tone Green Leaves
Matched—Casual, Kitchen and Ovenware, for Every Use.
Lovely Informal Table Service — Picnics — Parties — Teas — Rumpus Rooms, Etc.

76A—Cookie Jar or Bean Pot

246A—3-Pc. Deep Bowl Set
63A—2 Pt. Bowl
64A—4 Pt. Bowl
65A—6 Pt. Bowl

AB—5-Pc. Bowl Set
5A—5" Mixing Bowl
6A—6" Mixing Bowl
7A—7" Mixing Bowl
8A—8" Mixing Bowl
9A—9" Mixing Bowl

73A—9½" Salad

62A—½ Pt. Pitcher
16A—2 Pt. Pitcher
17A—5 Pt. Pitcher w/Guard

601AC—64 oz. Casserole and Cover

AN—5 Pc. Nappy Set
602A—4¾" 7 oz.
603A—5¾" 13 oz.
604A—6¾" 25 oz.
600A—7¾" 41 oz.
601A—8¾" 64 oz.

74A—5½" Ind. Salad or Cereal Bowl

503A—3½ Qt. Cookie Jar & Cover W/Handles

1963 catalog.

NO. 200 SALESMAN KIT ADVERTISING SPECIALTY ITEMS

This kit is an excellent way for your salesman to show customers the various items that can be imprinted, in various patterns. The pitcher shows Ad Copy on outside collar, the mixing bowls, and Covered Casseroles will have Ad Copy on inside bottom.

The kit measures 23¼" long, 9¼" wide, 7¼" deep, in a beautiful colored box. These are available with sample piece at a minimum cost.

WHEN ORDERING PLEASE STATE PATTERN DESIRED.

$5.25 each Net. F.O.B. FACTORY

MIXING BOWLS
With Imprint

PITCHERS
With Imprint

ADVERTISING SPECIALTY ITEMS

Watt Pottery Company
Crooksville,
Ohio

Salesman kit, year unknown.

STONEWARE SPECIALTY ITEMS

All Pieces Fired to 2000 Degrees Fahrenheit. Will Stand Heat or Cold, and will Retain These Temperatures Longer Than Ordinary Containers.

504—6 ½" Spaniel
Dog Dish
Yellow, Copper and
Turquoise

5" Kitty Dish
Turquoise
and Yellow

6" Dog Dish
7" Dog Dish
Brown and Green

75—8 oz. Open
Individual Bean Pot
77—16 oz. Open
Individual Bean Pot
Brown Only

76—2 Qt. Bean Pot
and Cover
93—1 ½ Qt. Bean Pot
and Cover
502—1 Gal. Bean Pot
and Cover
Above Brown Only
See Price List For Sets

No. 76G—64 oz.

No. 59G—80 oz.

No. 72G—96 oz.

No. 400-2—2 gallon
Tea Dispenser
No. 400-3—3 gallon
Tea Dispenser

Shown above with Tomlinson
No Drip Faucet. (Lever Type)
For trade name, see Price List.
No. 61-5.

1963 catalog.

WOOD-GRAIN
SERIES "W"

Rich Wood Grain Finish—Excellent For Outdoor Living—For the Kitchen—Oven to Table Service

WG—5 Pc. Bowl Set
605W—1 Pt. Mixing Bowl
606W—1 Qt. Mixing Bowl
607W—1 ½ Qt. Mixing Bowl
608W—2 ½ Qt. Mixing Bowl
610W—4 Qt. Mixing Bowl

613W—14 oz. Pitcher
614W—36 oz. Pitcher
615W—70 oz. Pitcher

608WC—72 oz. Dutch Oven

620W—9 ½" Salad Bowl

617W—6 qt. Cookie Barrel

6111W—4 Pc. Condiment Set

619W—5 ½" Ind. Salad Bowl

621W—Mug

625W—10" Plate

618W—88 oz. Bean Pot

1964 catalog.

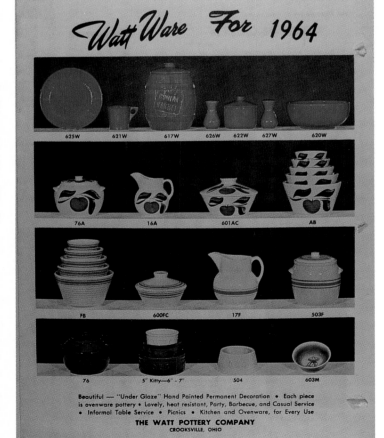

Watt Ware For 1964

625W	621W	617W	626W	622W	627W	620W
76A	16A	601AC				AB
FB	600FC	17F				503F
76	5" Kitty—6" - 7"		504			603M

Beautiful — "Under Glaze" Hand Painted Permanent Decoration • Each piece
is ovenware pottery • Lovely, heat resistant, Party, Barbecue, and Casual Service
• Informal Table Service • Picnics • Kitchen and Ovenware, for Every Use

THE WATT POTTERY COMPANY
CROOKSVILLE, OHIO

1964 catalog cover.

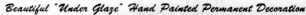

Beautiful "Under Glaze" Hand Painted Permanent Decoration
"RED APPLE"
SERIES "A"

Apple with Green Stem and Two Tone Green Leaves
Matched—Casual, Kitchen and Ovenware, for Every Use.
Lovely Informal Table Service — Picnics — Parties — Teas — Rumpus Rooms, Etc.

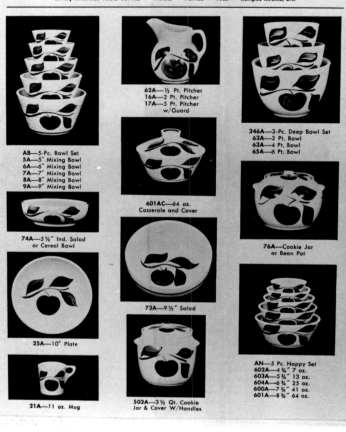

62A—½ Pt. Pitcher
16A—2 Pt. Pitcher
17A—5 Pt. Pitcher
w/Guard

AB—5-Pc. Bowl Set
5A—5" Mixing Bowl
6A—6" Mixing Bowl
7A—7" Mixing Bowl
8A—8" Mixing Bowl
9A—9" Mixing Bowl

246A—3-Pc. Deep Bowl Set
63A—2 Pt. Bowl
63A—4 Pt. Bowl
65A—6 Pt. Bowl

601AC—64 oz.
Casserole and Cover

74A—5½" Ind. Salad
or Cereal Bowl

76A—Cookie Jar
or Bean Pot

73A—9½" Salad

25A—10" Plate

21A—11 oz. Mug

503A—3½ Qt. Cookie
Jar & Cover W/Handles

AN—5 Pc. Nappy Set
602A—4¾" 7 oz.
603A—5¾" 13 oz.
604A—6¾" 25 oz.
600A—7¾" 41 oz.
601A—8¾" 64 oz.

1964 catalog.

STONEWARE SPECIALTY ITEMS

All Pieces Fired to 2000 Degrees Fahrenheit. Will Stand Heat or Cold, and will
Retain These Temperatures Longer Than Ordinary Containers.

75—8 oz. Open
Individual Bean Pot
77—16 oz. Open
Individual Bean Pot
Brown Only

5" Kitty Dish
Turquoise
and Yellow

6" Dog Dish
7" Dog Dish
Brown and Green

76—2 Qt. Bean Pot
and Cover
93—1½ Qt. Bean Pot
and Cover
502—1 Gal. Bean Pot
and Cover
Above Brown Only
See Price List For Sets

504—6½" Spaniel
Dog Dish
Yellow, Copper and
Turquoise

No. 400-2—2 gallon
Tea Dispenser
No. 400-3—3 gallon
Tea Dispenser

Shown above with Tomlinson
No Drip Faucet. (Lever Type)
For trade name, see Price List.
No. 64-4.

603M—Mexican
Chili Bowl

IMPORTANT NOTICE

Breakage should be reported to the transportation company at once and claim
made to them. If the package has been signed for, as having been received in good condition, your claim should be made for "concealed damage."

Duplicate receipts which should accompany your claim will be furnished upon request. The goods were PACKED WITH GREAT CARE by experienced packers and
we cannot assume responsibility for breakage occurring in transit.

NO ALLOWANCE FOR BREAKAGE

1964 catalog.

Footnotes

1. A search of all available issues of The Crockery and Glass Journal
and other publications of the pottery industry revealed advertisements
(for Watt ware), placed by the George Borgfeldt Corporation, but
none by the Watt Pottery itself. These publications featured an index
to all advertisers, making a search reasonably thorough.
2. A detailed listing of the pieces produced was kept by W.I. Watt.
This listing included the mold identification numbers and a description of each piece, the number produced and the identification of the
decorative stamp used on each piece.

Chapter 3
Stoneware Age
1922-1935

Stoneware from this period was found on a variety of utilitarian shapes. (See Chapter 2 for catalogs.) The Acorn mark was
used from 1926 until the early 1930s. The Eagle mark was in
use by 1933. Stoneware production halted in 1935.

Eagle crocks. 10 gallon white, 6 gallon two-tone.

5 gallon Eagle crock, two-tone.

10 gallon, white, Eagle crock with handles. 2
gallon Acorn crock, two-tone.

Handled crocks. 8 gallon, white Eagle. 12 gallon, white Acorn.

5 gallon, two-tone Acorn jug. 6 gallon, two-tone Acorn crock.

6 gallon, white Acorn handled crock. 5 gallon, white Acorn jug.

5 gallon, two-tone eagle jug, 5 gallon, white Eagle handled crock.

4 gallon Acorn churn.

4 gallon white, Eagle crock. 4 gallon, two-tone Acorn preserve jar.

Blue-banded, Acorn water coolers. 10 gallon and 3 gallon.

Chapter 4
Early Kitchen & Oven Ware 1935-Mid 1940s

The ware from this period is found on a small number of different shapes. Most shapes have a heavy shoulder around the upper rim. This shoulder is unglazed on the top and bottom to allow stacking in the kiln without the pieces firing together. Patterns from this period were officially known by numbers, instead of pattern names. Descriptive names are used by today's collectors.

Most early kitchen and oven ware is well marked with the "Oven Ware - Made In U.S.A." bottom mark. Some pieces only have the size marked. (See Chapter 32 for bottom marks.) The Moon and Stars pattern is often not marked at all. Pieces in this pattern can be found with Watt, foil stickers on the bottom. We are attributing the Moon and Stars pattern to the Watt Pottery because of the similarity in the shapes, and the glazes.

Mixing bowls and casseroles are the same diameters. Mixing bowls are frequently found today with lids, which they did not come with. The casserole bowls are much lower in profile than the mixing bowls. Actual sizes of the bowls are about one-half of an inch bigger than the size as marked. (A #7 bowl measures 7 1/2" in diameter.)

Early kitchen and oven ware pieces were designed so that they could be stacked during firing.

Loops mixing bowls, assorted colors, 5" through 9".

#9 Loops casseroles.

Loops lug casseroles in assorted colors, 5".

Arcs #8 and #7 casseroles, tan.

Arcs #10 dome-top roaster, tan.

Moon & Stars and Arcs custard cups, 3 1/2" dia, 2 1/2" h.

Arcs #8 casserole, #9 mixing bowl, white/brown bands.

Arcs #7 casserole, #5 mixing bowl, white bands.

#8 pie plates. Brown Loops, tan and blue Arcs.

Raised Button lug casseroles, assorted colors, 5".

Green Moon & Stars, 8" casserole and pie plate; 3" and 4" bowls.

Tan Moon & Stars casseroles, 8" and 6".

Tan Arcs, and Moon & Stars canisters. 7" dia. 7 1/2" h.
(Moon & Stars canister has Art Deco columns, but no moon
or stars.)

Tan Moon & Stars mixing
bowls, 10", 9", 8", 6".

Tan Moon & Stars pitcher, 5 1/2" dia, 6 1/2" h. Creamer has similar design (Watt?) 3" dia, 4 1/2" h.

Green Moon & Stars small pitcher, 3 1/2" dia, 4 1/2" h. Tan 5" bowl.

Old style bean pot and Diamond bowls, 4 1/2". Boxed set packed with 1942 Zanesville newspapers.

#8 tan Diamond casserole.

Bak-Ezee casserole, 9" dia, 7 1/2" h.

Bak-Ezee bowl, 7"; pie plate, 8".

Chapter 5
Transitional Ware 1943-1950

Until the early 1940s, the Watt Pottery produced ware which was characterized by simple, old fashioned shapes. Most of these early kitchen and oven ware pieces had heavy rims. By 1943, the pottery undertook the production of more modern ware, much of which was proprietary ware for large distributors. Thus, the Watt Pottery began the transition from old-fashioned ware to the pieces which were hand-decorated in the 1950s. By the end of the decade, the Eve-N-Bake line and other banded ware bore the same shapes that would become the classic pattern ware of the early 1950s.

Lug-handled casseroles, 4 1/4" and 8 1/2" diameters. These pieces, which resemble certain Russel Wright designs, are among the oldest pieces which were not the early kitchen and oven ware style (see Chapter 4). They are marked with typical 1940s bottom marks.

EMBOSSED WREATH

The correct name for this pattern is not known. It was referred to as a "dainty wreath" by W.I. Watt in a 1986 article. It was produced in 1943 and distributed through the George Borgfeldt Corporation.

#5 and #9 Embossed Wreath nappies.

Advertisement for Embossed Wreath ware. Reprinted from the *Crockery and Glass Journal*, June, 1943

#6 Embossed Wreath nappy in light blue.

KLA-HAM'RD

Produced in 1944, this line was made to resemble hammered aluminum ware. Kla-Ham'rd means, "clay - hammered". All pieces have a unique bottom mark. (See Chapter 32 for bottom mark.)

Kla-Ham'rd #43-14 pitchers, 7 1/2" h, 4 1/2" dia.

Kla-Ham'rd stacking refrigerator pitchers. Marked: S, M, L; 4 1/4", 4 3/4" and 5" dia.

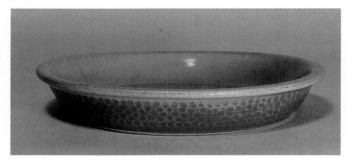

Kla-Ham'rd #43-13 pie plate, 9" dia.

Kla-Ham'rd mixing bowls, #43-15, #43-16, #43-17; 6 1/2", 8", 10" dia.

Kla-Ham'rd #43-18 bean pot, 9" dia, 5 1/2" h.

Possibly the predecessor to Kla-Ham'rd, this small bowl has a regular 1940s Watt bottom mark, not a Kla-Ham'rd mark; 5" dia, 2 1/2" h.

Kla-Ham'rd casseroles, left to right: #43-12, 9" dia. 4" h, 7 1/2" h w/ lid; #43-11, 8 1/2" dia, 3 3/4" h, 5 1/4" h w/lid; #43-4-6, 7 1/2" dia, 3 1/2" h, 4" h w/lid.

Some Kla-Ham'rd pieces are found with or without lids and lug handles. Rear, #43-8-10, 8 3/4" dia, 3" h; Front, #43-2, 5" dia, 2 3/4" h.

CABINART

The Cabinart trade name was listed in the *Crockery and Glass Journal* annual directory in 1944 and 1945 both by the Watt Pottery and the George Borgfeldt Corporation. Most pieces of Cabinart are two-tone brown. A few are found in solid brown, and rarer still, aqua glaze. All pieces have a Cabinart bottom mark.

Some ware which is identical to Cabinart is marked "American Homes". This name was registered to Promotions Incorporated. The authors have only found a few different molds marked this way, mostly mixing bowls. (See Chapter 32 for Cabinart and American Homes bottom marks.)

Cabinart covered creamer and sugar bowl. Both 3 1/2" h.

Cabinart stacking creamers come in several sizes. 4" dia, 3" h and 4 1/2" dia, 3 3/4" h.

Cabinart pitchers (left to right); 7 1/2" h, ice-lip pitchers, two-tone and solid brown; 6" h, pitcher, two-tone.

Cabinart jars come in many sizes. 6" dia, 8" h and 8 1/4" dia, 4 1/2" h.

Cabinart bakers come with or without handles. Both 6 1/2" dia, 4 1/2" h.

Cabinart pie plate and 4" custard cups. Aqua colored Cabinart pieces are hard to find.

Left to right: Cabinart 10" mixing bowl, American Homes 9" mixing bowl.

SWIRL

The official name for this pattern is not known. We refer to it as "Swirl". At first glance, this pattern from the 1940s appears the same as Kolor Kraft from the 1950s. These are not the same molds, however. The ribs on Kolor Kraft curve continuously in one direction. The ribs on Swirl pieces, begin curving one way, and half-way down the side of the bowl they begin curving in the opposite direction.

Swirl bowls have either a rounded lip with no shoulder, or a lip and a very short shoulder. Kolor Kraft bowls have a flared lip on a long shoulder, or just a shoulder with no lip.

Comparison between Swirl (1940s) and Kolor Kraft (1950s). The ribs on the blue Swirl bowl are more re-curved than the yellow Kolor Kraft bowl. The lip on the Swirl bowl is more rounded, while the Kolor Kraft bowl has a shoulder, and the lip is flared.

The 1940s Watt solid color glazes are beautifully done. 5" through 8" Swirl mixing bowls.

Swirl #9 pie plates, blue and tan.

These mixing bowls are from the late 1940s time period. They have been given a shoulder (shorter than Kolor Kraft's) but their rib design and bottom marks clearly define them as Swirl.

#7 Swirl casserole, rose, 7 1/4" dia, 4" h w/lid.

PEEDEECO

This actually a trade name rather than a pattern name, which stands for Pitman-Dreitzer and Company of New York. All pieces resemble pumpkins in shape and color. There are only five different pieces known to the authors. Peedeeco pieces have their own bottom marks. (See Chapter 32.)

Peedeeco 5-pint pitcher and bean pot, 4" bean cups.

Peedeeco 5" and 8" lug casseroles.

EVE-N-BAKE

This is a Watt trade name registered in 1946. There are two patterns unique to Eve-N-Bake pieces: (1) thin, brown, sprayed bands at the top and bottom of all pieces, and (2) three heavy bands of white slip over yellow-ware colored glaze. All pieces have a series of raised ridges just above the bottom of the ware. Covered pieces have ridges on the lids, also. All pieces have an Eve-N-Bake bottom mark. (See Chapter 32.) Occasionally, a piece of Rio Rose or other pattern ware will have the Eve-N-Bake bottom mark.

Eve-N-Bake pitcher, 7" h. White bands on yellow.

Eve-N-Bake casserole, 8"; and bakers, 5", 6 1/2", and 8" dia. White bands on yellow.

Eve-N-Bake deep mixing bowls. 10" dia, 6 1/2" h and 6 1/2" dia, 5 1/2" h. White bands on yellow.

Eve-N-Bake pitcher, 7" h.; mand #21 cookie jar. Spray brown bands.

Eve-N-Bake casseroles, 8" and 6 1/2" dia. Spray brown bands.

Eve-N-Bake domed casseroles, 9" dia, 6 1/2" h w/lid and 8" dia, 6" h w/lid. Spray brown bands.

Eve-N-Bake lug casseroles, 5" and 8" dia. Spray brown bands.

Eve-N-Bake mixing bowls, 8" and 6". Spray brown bands.

MISCELLANEOUS BANDED WARE

These pieces resemble the Eve-N-Bake ware, except the embossed ridges characteristic of the Eve-N-Bake line have been eliminated. The mixing bowls from this period are deeper than the later mixing bowl series.

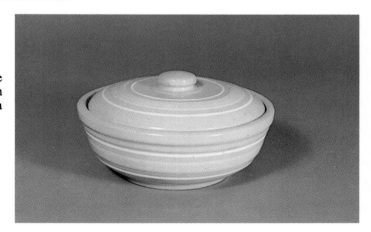

Casserole, 7 1/2". Light blue/white bands.

Mixing bowls, 5" to 8". Light blue/white bands.

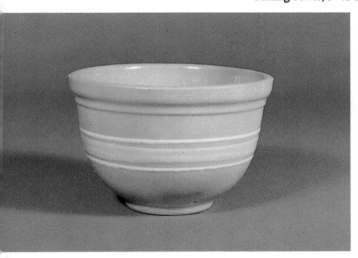

Deep mixing bowl, 6 1/2" dia, 4 1/4" h. Light blue/white bands.

#21 cookie jar, old style pitcher. Light blue/white bands.

Brown banded mixing bowls; 6 1/4" deep bowl, 8 1/4" deep bowl, 10" regular bowl. These are heavy bands of slip, not the thin, brush-decorated bands of Par-T-Que from the late 1950s.

Brown banded #1 bowls.

Deep mixing bowls. 8" brown/white bands, 6 1/4" black/white bands.

Chapter 6
Classic Patterns
1949-1953

In 1949, the Watt Pottery began the production of the first hand-decorated ware. These original patterns were produced for only a few years, and most were probably out of production by 1952 when Apple was introduced. Rio Rose, the longest lasting Classic pattern, is found on a few newer shapes, such as the #15, #16, and #17 pitchers and 50 series bowls. Classic patterned ware is characterized by the following features:

(1) The mold shapes.

    (a) Classic pattern ware can be commonly found on table service, such as plates, cups and saucers.

    (b) All of the casseroles feature lids recessed into the bowl.

    (c) These patterns can all be found on the old style pitcher.

(2) Complex leaves.

    Most Classic pattern ware has either incised veins on the leaves, or painted veins on the leaves. This practice probably proved to be too time consuming and error-prone. We have included Daisy as a Classic pattern because of the mold shapes it is found on. With its two-tone green leaves, Daisy is essentially a transition into the Modern patterns.

The pattern we call "Raised Rose" is an interesting one. It is presumably the oldest hand-decorated pattern. While it is indeed hand-decorated, it is not decorated *free-hand*, as the raised pattern served as a guide to apply the colored glaze. Although it has been widely reported that the raised flowers were applied to the finished bowls, the pieces we have examined all seem to be molded.

The beautiful Tropical pattern may only have been produced on a trial basis because only a very few pieces can be found today. It is the most complex of all the Classic patterns.

#48 stacking refrigerator set, Raised Rose.

Raised Rose casseroles. A pair of old style, oval handled, individual casseroles and an 8" casserole.

Each refrigerator pitcher came with a lid which allowed the next pitcher to stack atop it.

Raised Rose mixing bowls, 7" (2-leaf), and 9" (4-leaf); and baker, 8" (2-leaf).

RIO ROSE

Old style pitchers. Left: Rio Rose. Right: 4-leaf Raised Rose.

Rio Rose countertop display carton. *Courtesy of Duke and Nina Frash.*

Reprinted from the *Crockery and Glass Journal*, June, 1951.

Rio Rose modern pitchers, left to right: #15, #16, #17 plain lip.

#72 Rio Rose canister.

Two #21 cookie jars. Left: Raised Rose (4-leaf). Right: Rio Rose.

Rio Rose casseroles, left to right: 8" casserole, #20 roaster, #2/48 casserole.

A pair of individual, Rio Rose lug casseroles. Left: #18 grooved handle. Right: old style casserole, oval handled.

Rio Rose cups and saucers. Left: large cup and #27 saucer. Right: #40 cup, #41 saucer.

Rio Rose large cup, #27 saucer and sugar bowl.

Rio Rose mixing bowls, 5" through 9".

Comparison of #27 Rio Rose saucers for the large cup. Left to right: Deep #27 saucer, flat #27 saucer.

Rio Rose individual bowls, top to bottom: #4, #23, #22, #1, #52.

Rio Rose plates, left to right: #31 (15") platter, #49 (12") chop plate, #28 (7 1/2") plate, #42 (6 1/2") plate.

Rio Rose spaghetti bowls. Rear, left to right: #39 straight side, #25, #39 lipped. Front: #24.

Left to right: Rio Rose #23 salad bowl, Rio Rose #44 flat soup, Bullseye #22 berry bowl

#31 platter, #28 plate, 7 1/2", large cup and #27 deep saucer, Bullseye.

#30 snack plate with offset cup ring, 11 1/4"; #28 plate, Bullseye, 7 1/2".

Rear, left to right: #25 spaghetti bowl, #24 spaghetti bowl. Front: #33 pie plate, Bullseye.

Bullseye bowls. Rear: two different #44 flat soup bowls. Front: #25 spaghetti bowl.

TROPICAL

#4 Tropical bowl.

The historic first advertisement the Watt Pottery placed for hand-decorated ware, for the illusive Tropical pattern. Reprinted from the *Crockery and Glass Journal*, December, 1949.

Tropical dinner plate, 10".

STARFLOWER

As Starflower was introduced, it had six complex petals and incised veins on the leaves. Reprinted from the *Crockery and Glass Journal*, December, 1950.

Original Starflower #45 and #46 shakers.

Three-piece range set combines large, easy-to-grasp salt and pepper with utility jar which can hold either sugar or, with an eye to wartime shortages, used fats. Decorated in Starflower pattern, handpainted under the glaze. $2.98 set. Watt.

#31 platter in original Starflower, custom decorated by Jackie Sherrick.

Black Moonflower #39 spaghetti bowl and #22 berry bowl.

Graceful pink floral designs, hand-painted underglaze on a black body, are features of the Moonflower pattern. 20-piece set, $10.95. Watt.

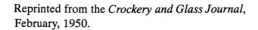

Reprinted from the *Crockery and Glass Journal*, February, 1950.

#31 platter, #101 plate, black Moonflower.

#40 cup and #41 saucer, black Moonflower.

Black Moonflower casseroles, left to right: #18 grooved handle, old style, oval handle.

Black Moonflower large creamer and sugar bowl.

Left to right: old style, oval handle casserole, #101 plate, #21 cookie jar, black Moonflower.

Left to right: 8" casserole, old style, oval handle casserole, #21 cookie jar, green Moonflower.

Wooden carousel with #8 casserole and #4 individual bowls, green Moonflower.

#40 cup, #41 saucer, #35 creamer and sugar bowl, green Moonflower.

#42 plate, 6 1/2"; #101 plate, #40 cup and #41 saucer, green Moonflower.

#31 platter, #101 plate, #18 groove handle casserole, green Moon-flower.

DOGWOOD

#24 spaghetti bowl and #4 individual bowls, green Moonflower.

Dogwood #24 spaghetti bowl and old style, oval handled casserole.

Dogwood #31 platter, #42 plate.

CROSS-HATCH PANSY

#21 cookie jar, Cross-Hatch Pansy.

Cross-Hatch Pansy pitchers, left to right: old style, #16, #15.

#18 grooved handle casserole, Cross-Hatch Pansy.

Cross-Hatch Pansy #40 cup.

Rear, left to right: #39 spaghetti bowl, #31 platter. Front, left to right: #33 pie plate, #43 (8 1/2") plate, Cross-Hatch Pansy.

#39 Cross-Hatch Pansy spaghetti bowl.

Cross-Hatch Pansy mixing bowls, 5", 7", 9".

Daisy plates, #43 (8 1/2"), #42 (6 1/2").

Daisy pie plate.

Daisy #40 cup and #41 saucer.

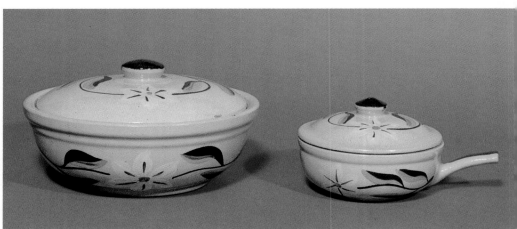

Daisy casseroles, #8 and old style, oval handled.

DAISY

#24 spaghetti bowl and four #23 individual bowls.

Chapter 7
Starflower

Starflower was the only pattern to be born as a Classic Pattern and evolve into one of the Modern Patterns. As a Classic Pattern, the original Starflower featured six petals on the flower and a fairly complex petal shape with rays painted on them. The leaves had incised veins, a characteristic of Classic Patterns. A bud on a stem completed the pattern.

By 1952, Starflower had been reduced to five petals with a simpler petal shape, and plain leaves. Starflower underwent a further reduction around 1959, when it appeared with four petals and no bud. We have not seen Starflower on the ribbed 600 series or the ribbed mixing bowls. This would indicate that Starflower was out of production by 1962.

A few Starflower molds were also decorated with different color combinations: red, blue or green backgrounds which have a white flower. These patterns always have four petals, and we refer to them as "Special Starflower." With only a single color used for the design, Special Starflower is the most reduced flower pattern. They are most commonly found on the #39 spaghetti bowl.

There is a modern version of Starflower which had six petals. This has been found on #76 bean pots. The pattern has no bud, but the flower is repeated on the back of the bean pot as well as the front. The "ear" handles on the bean pot are green. This pattern is easily distinguished from the original Starflower pattern.

Star Flower, a red and green floral design on a buff-colored body, decorates this 2-quart Dutch oven. $1.89 retail. Watt Pottery Co., Crooksville, Ohio.

Starflower advertisement. Reprinted from the *Crockery and Glass Journal*, February, 1955

5-petal #69 refrigerator pitcher.

4-petal #72 canister. (No lid).

4-petal pitchers. Left to right: #69, #62 creamer, #15, #16, #17 ice-lip.

5-petal pitchers. Left to right: #17 plain lip, #16, #15, #62 creamer.

Left to right: #56 curved side tumblers, 5-petal. #501 4-petal mugs. #61 5-petal mugs.

4 and 5-petal #62 creamers, 5-petal #98 sugar bowl.

Modern range set. 4-petal #117 and #118 hourglass shakers, #01 grease jar.

Old-style range set. 5-petal #45 and #46 barrel shakers, #47 grease jar.

#115 4-petal coffee carafe.

#80 4-petal cheese crock.

4-petal #96 covered baker on stand.

4-petal #8182 canister set.

#67 covered bakers, 4 and 5-petal.

4-petal #503 cookie jar.

4-petal #76 bean pot, #75 bean cups.

4-petal #18 tab handle.

Rear, left to right: 5-petal #31 platter, #49 chop plate. Front: 4-petal #33 pie plate.

5-petal #25 spaghetti bowl, #18 grooved handle casserole.

5-petal #21 cookie jar, 4-petal #76 bean pot.

4 and 5-petal #59 ice buckets.

Top to bottom: 5-petal #52, #53, #54 bowls.

5-petal 8" old-style baker, #18 tab handle casserole.

#64 deep mixing bowls, 4 and 5-petal.

5-petal salad set in display box. This set consists of a #24 salad bowl and four #52 individual bowls.

#50 5-petal bowl.

#60 5-petal, inside decoration.

Rear, left to right: #55 salad bowl, #73 salad bowl. Front: #4 salad bowls.

Left to right: 5-petal #67, #66, #60, #68 bowls.

4-petal #04, #05, #06, #07 nappies.

#15 black on white Starflower. (Probably a test piece).

Special Starflower #07 nappy, white flower on blue background.

5-petal mixing bowls, #5 through #9.

Special Starflower #39 spaghetti bowls, white flower on red, green and blue background.

Special Starflower #24 spaghetti bowl, white 5-petal flower on green background, no bud.

Special Starflower #39 spaghetti bowl, white flower on turquoise background.

Special Starflower #39 spaghetti bowl, orange 5-petal flower on spray brown background.

Chapter 8
Apple

Red Apple, as it was officially known, was introduced in January, 1952. It proved to be the Watt Pottery's best selling pattern, and was still in production at the pottery's end in 1965. There are two main versions of the pattern. Three-leaf Apple (with two-tone leaves), was the only version ever featured in the catalogs or advertisements. Two-leaf Apple, which has only a single green color on the leaves, is a variation which was probably made available at a reduced cost. Apple pieces cannot be dated by the number of leaves, or by the shading on the leaves.

Another variation is the pattern called "Reduced Apple" by collectors. This is a very simple pattern comprised of an apple with no stem, and two simple leaves. The final variation is referred to as "Open Apple." Much different than the regular Apple pattern, it has been included in this chapter because it does feature an apple. Note: Double Apple is a separate pattern featured in chapter 16.

The Apple pattern is found on the widest variety of molds of any pattern. The earliest pieces, from 1952, can be found on Classic Pattern molds such as the #20, 10 1/2" roaster. Apple remained in production through all of the style changes in the Watt lineup and can be found on all bowl styles, from the 50 series through the 600 series.

Left to right: #505 32-ounce tea pot, #115 60-ounce covered coffee server, #112 6-cup tea pot.

The introductory advertisement for Apple. To the author's knowledge, no one has found one of the "always popular Cookie Jars." Reprinted from the *Crockery and Glass Journal*, December, 1951.

#62 creamers, 2-leaf and 3-leaf. #98 3-leaf covered sugar bowl.

3-leaf mugs, left to right: #701, #501, #121. A #61 mug was also made.

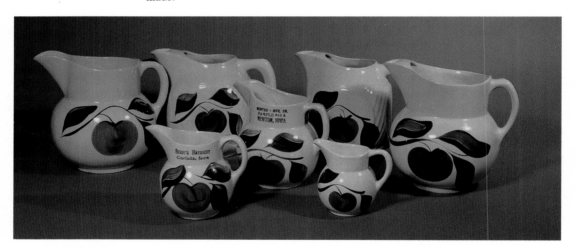

Rear, left to right: #17 3-leaf plain-lip, #69 3-leaf, #69 2-leaf, #17 3-leaf ice-lip. Front, left to right: #15 3-leaf, #16 3-leaf, #62 2-leaf.

A few Apple mugs are found with advertising, like this #701.

3-leaf shakers, left to right: #117 & #118 hourglass shakers ("S" and "P" holes), #45 & #46 barrel shakers, #117 & #118 hourglass shakers (raised "S" and "P").

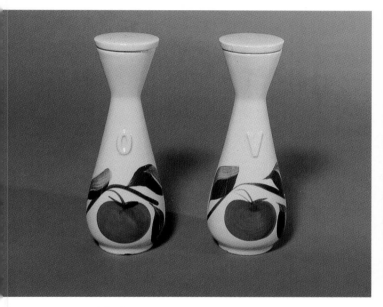

#126 cruets, 3-leaf.

Apple advertising salesman's samples: #126 cruets, #31 Platter, #17 ice-lip pitcher. Below: #62 creamer.

Most Apple divided dinner plates are found with this reduced pattern.

Left to right: #49 chop plate, #31 platter, #101 dinner plate, all 3-leaf Apple.

#29 3-leaf dinner plates with advertising.

#29 3-leaf dinner plate advertising salesman's samples.

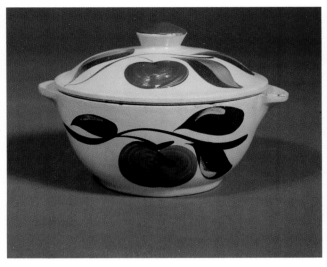

3-leaf #49 chop plate and #29 dinner plate, with advertising.

#18 tab handle casserole, 3-leaf.

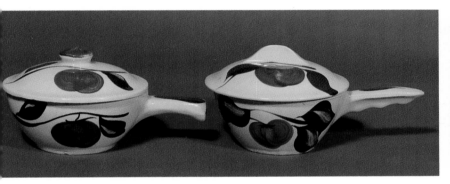

Left: #18 groove handle casserole, button knob. Right: #18 French handle casserole, blade knob.

The Watt Pottery sold the #18 tab handle casserole with the #01 lid in 1959.

2-leaf Apple #8182 canister set.

3-leaf Apple #8182 canister set.

The #18 French handle casserole was also sold with the button knob on the lid.

#72 canisters, 2 and 3-leaf.

Left to right: #01 (modern) grease jar, #82 canister, #47 (early) grease jar.

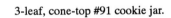
3-leaf, cone-top #91 cookie jar.

3-leaf #80 cheese crock.

2-leaf, cone-top #91 cookie jar.

#02 3-leaf refrigerator set (one section missing).

2-leaf #85 rectangular baker, #84 3-leaf square covered casserole.

#21 cookie jar, 3-leaf.

Left to right: 3-leaf #76 bean pot, 3-leaf #503 cookie jar, 2-leaf #76 bean pot.

Two sizes of bean pots have been found in apple. Left: #502 4-quart.
Right: #76 2 1/2 quart.

2 and 3-leaf #59 ice buckets.

The most common chip-n-dip set, the #1219, consists of a #119 dip bowl, a #120 chip bowl, and a metal rack with a hoop 3 1/2" inside diameter.

An early chip-n-dip set was the #0596, with an #05 dip bowl, a #96 chip bowl, and a metal rack with a hoop measuring nearly 5" inside diameter. These were sold through the Signet Club Plan.

A third chip-n-dip set was the #6012, with a #602 dip bowl and a #601 chip bowl. The rack pictured has a small shelf for the dip bowl to rest on and has a 4 1/2" inside diameter hoop.

Left to right: #67 and #66 covered bakers, 3-leaf.

#67 covered baker, 2-leaf.

Early 3-leaf casseroles. Left: #3/19 (actually just the #19, but they are marked 3/19 for some reason). Right: #2/48.

Left to right: #600 and #601 covered bakers on wire racks, 3-leaf.

#20 roaster, 3-leaf.

#70 Dutch oven, 2-leaf.

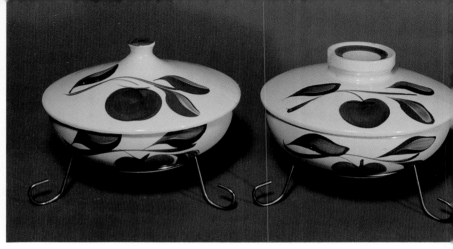

#96 3-leaf bakers on wire racks, large and small knobs on lids.

#73 covered salad bowls. The cover only goes on a bowl with outside decoration, either apples or just a green band. The #73 salad bowl with the apple on the inside is not covered.

#110 covered baker on a #133 solid-base, electric warmer.

2-leaf #3/19 with candle warmer in a boxed set.

3-leaf salad set. #73 salad bowl and #74 small salad bowls.

2-leaf salad set. #73 salad bowl and #74 small salad bowls.

(4) #23 bowls and an 8" baker, 3-leaf.

Rear, left to right: 2-leaf #39, 3-leaf #25, 3-leaf #24 spaghetti bowls.
Front: #44 3-leaf flat soup, inside band.

Two styles of 3-leaf #44 flat soup bowls, inside and outside band.
The inside banded bowl is harder to find.

Left: 3-leaf #24 spaghetti bowl, Right: 2-leaf #39 straight sided,
spaghetti bowl.

3-leaf #50 bowl.

3-leaf mixing bowl set, #5 through #9.

2-leaf mixing bowls, #6 through #9.

2-leaf deep mixing bowls. Left: #65. Right: #63.

#106 salad bowl, 3-leaf.

3-leaf ribbed mixing bowl set, #5 through #9.

3-leaf nappies, #04 through #07.

#33 3-leaf pie plates. (Rack is not a Watt piece.)

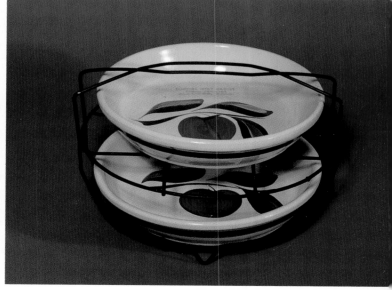

3-leaf deep mixing bowls. Top to bottom: #63, #64, #65.

3-leaf #95 and #96 bakers.

Left to right: #60, #66, #67, 2-leaf

Open Apple covered bakers. Left: #110. Right: #96. The funnel lid was designed for the #110. The lid was fitted to the #96 to make a covered baker out of it.

Two hard to find bowls in the Apple pattern. Left: #1. Right: #75 bean cup.

3-leaf ribbed bakers. Left to right: #602, #603, #604, #600, #601.

Reduced Apple bowls. Top to bottom: #61, #63, #64, #65 deep mixing bowls. Left and right: #74. These are the only pieces we have found in Reduced Apple.

Open Apple nappies. Left to right: #04, #05, #06, #07.

Open Apple #62 creamer.

Open Apple #39 spaghetti bowl.

Open Apple mixing bowls, #5, #6, #8.

Open Apple #73 salad bowl.

Chapter 9
Silhouette

Silhouette was derived in 1953 from the Starflower pattern by spraying a light brown background on the clay body, then hand painting the pattern in chartreuse glaze. The design of the pattern is typical 5-petal Starflower. The Watt Pottery placed more advertisements for Silhouette than any other pattern we could locate, even informing buyers about production delays during the introduction of the pattern. It is found on a fairly small number of molds.

#31 platter, #18 tab handle casserole.

Silhouette advertisement. Reprinted from the *Crockery and Glass Journal*, December, 1952.

#15, #16, #17 plain-lip pitchers.

#9 and #5 mixing bowls.

#21 cookie jar.

#4 individual salad bowl, #54 baker.

Chapter 10
Cherry

We have not found the introduction date of Cherry, but from the molds it is found on, it is an early pattern. The newest molds we have seen it on are the 50 series bakers, but we have not seen it on the old style pitcher. This dates Cherry between 1951 and 1954, we suspect towards the earlier date.

#45 and #46 barrel salt and pepper shakers. Cherry salt shakers were sold primarily with the popcorn set. This is the only Cherry pepper shaker the authors located.

#52 bowl with inside pattern, #31 platter. These may have been sold together as a chip-n-dip set.

#17 plain lip, #16, #15 pitchers.

#56 straight sided tumbler.

2/48 casserole.

#53 and #54 covered bakers.

Popcorn set in display box and companion #55 popcorn bowl.

#52, #53, #54 bakers.

#39 and #24 spaghetti bowls, #18 groove handle casserole.

#49 platter, #25 spaghetti bowl.

#31 platter, #49 chop plate with unusual flower.

#21 cookie jar.

Chapter 11
Rooster

The Rooster pattern was introduced in 1955. It must have been produced through 1958 as it is found on the hourglass shakers. Rooster pieces sold for about 5% more than Apple pieces during the same year, probably due to the higher decorating cost. The shapes of the rooster vary more than any other Watt pattern, from skinny to decidedly chubby. While it was once thought that the individual decorators might be responsible for the different rooster shapes, interviews with the decorators produced the response, "We made them depending on how we felt that day!"

Like the Dutch Tulip pattern, no #17 Rooster pitcher has been located to our knowledge, nor do the decorators remember making any. It remains a Holy Grail among Watt collectors.

#98 covered sugar, #62 creamer, with advertising.

#117 and #118 hourglass shakers ("S" and "P" holes), #45 and #46 barrel shakers.

Reprinted from the *Crockery and Glass Journal*, December, 1954.

◆ *Watt Pottery Co.*

A contemporary new shape, with two new decorations, is being brought to market by Watt Pottery, Crooksville, O.

Both patterns (one a rooster in red and black, with green accents; the other a band-decoration in pink and turquoise) are available in a 4-piece nappy set ($1.98), two covered casseroles ($1.29 each), cookie jar ($1.29), salad bowl ($1.50) and in ½ pint, 1 pint and 2 pint pitchers.

It's all ovenware and it's all handpainted.

CROCKERY & GLASS JOURNAL for December, 1954

Left to right: #62 creamer, #15, #16, and #69 pitchers.

#61 mug.

#80 cheese crock.

#18 French-handled casserole, button knob.

Left to right: #59 ice bucket, #76 cookie jar.

#86 oval casserole, #85 rectangular baker.

#66 and #67 covered bakers.

#05 covered nappy.

#70 Dutch oven.

#39 straight-sided spaghetti bowl.

#33 pie plate.

Left to right: #68, #60, #66, #67 bowls.

Mixing bowls, #5 through #9.

Ribbed mixing bowls, #7 and #5.

Deep mixing bowls. Top to bottom: #63, #64, #65.

#58 fruit bowl.

Chapter 12
Dutch Tulip

This pattern was introduced in 1956 as the "Pennsylvania Dutch" line, but is more commonly known today as Dutch Tulip. Dutch Tulip is found on different molds than the regular Tulip pattern, which was sold six years later. One of the Dutch Tulip pieces which collectors have been searching for is the #17 pitcher. To our knowledge, none has been found. The Watt decorators did not recall making any #17 Dutch Tulip pitchers.

Gay Pennsylvania Dutch design on these stoneware cannisters is a colorful kitchen brightener. $3.70 ret. for set of 4. Watt Pottery Co., Crooksville, O.

Reprinted from the *Crockery and Glass Journal*, February, 1956.

Divided dinner plate, #45 and #46 barrel shakers.

Left to right: #69, #16, #15, #62.

#61 mug.

#85 rectangular baker.

#8182 canister set.

Left to right: #76 cookie jar, #59 ice bucket, #80 cheese crock.

#72 Canister.

#18 French-handled casserole.

An interesting variation on a #74 individual bowl.

#39 spaghetti bowl.

Rear, left to right: #67, #66 covered bakers. Front: #68 baker.

Left to right: #65, #64, #63 deep mixing bowls.

#73 salad bowls.

Chapter 13
American Red Bud

American Red Bud was featured in the 1957 Watt catalog, and is usually called "Tear Drop" by today's collectors (even W.I. Watt called it Tear Drop in *Collectibles*). Tear Drop is the collectors' best bet to find a rectangular baker, or the square or oval covered casseroles.

Some Tear Drop bean pots are found with decorated lids.

#69, #16, #15 pitchers, #62 creamer.

#117 and #118 hourglass shakers, raised "S" & "P". #45 and #46 barrel shakers.

#76 bean pot and #75 bean cups. Bean cups have only 2 buds instead of 3.

Very unusual bean pot set with yellow over-glaze.

#05, #06, #07 nappies, #05 covered nappy.

#73 salad bowl, #74 individual salads.

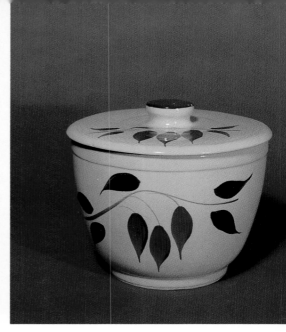

#59 ice bucket.

#84 square baker.

#68 bakers. (Part of 68, 60 ,66, 67 set.)

#39 spaghetti bowl.

#18 French handle casserole, #85 rectangular baker.

#5, #7, #9 mixing bowls.

#63, #64, #65 deep mixing bowls.

#82 Coffee and Tea canisters (Flour and Sugar missing), #72 canister.

Chapter 14
Morning Glory

The Morning Glory pattern was sold in 1958, and is the Watt Pottery's second embossed, hand-decorated pattern (Raised Rose was the first). There are three color schemes: regular Watt red and green, a yellow-glazed version, and brown and cream. As introduced, Morning Glory had a different look. The flower on the left was turned to face straight out, rather than to the side. (See the catalog reprint section). To the authors' knowledge, none of these pieces have been found, and production may have been limited to the display pieces at the trade shows. There are only 11 different pieces in the Morning Glory line.

Morning Glory advertising #98 sugar.

Left to right: #97 creamer, #96 ice-lip pitcher, #98 sugar bowl. No lids are known for the sugar bowl.

Yellow glazed #98 sugar, #97 creamer.

Mixing bowls, #7, #8, #9.

Yellow glazed #94 covered baker, 8 1/2" dia, 4" h, 6 1/2" h w/lid.

Yellow glazed #9 mixing bowl.

Brown/cream #95 cookie jar. 10 3/4" h.

NOT-WATT! These pieces are made by the Robinson-Ransbottom Pottery Company (R.R.P.Co.). These pieces are often mistaken for Watt, particularly the morning glory pattern. There are several other patterns similar to these three. The leaf color in this hand-decorated R.R.P.Co. ware is a dark blue-green. This ware is seldom marked, although an occasional piece can be found with R.R.P.Co.'s "crown" mark on the bottom. Small canisters and the pictured cookie jar are the most common pieces of R.R.P.Co. to be found.

Chapter 15
Autumn Foliage

This is the simplest Watt pattern with only a single color of glaze used. Autumn Foliage was introduced in 1959. Autumn Foliage and Apple are the only patterns that we have found on the #115 carafe and both tea pots, which were new shapes in 1959. The Autumn Foliage carafe is the ribbon handled version with no lid, while Apple is found on the small handled, covered coffee server.

CASSEROLE and cover on ceramic stand, electrified. Retails for $3.98. Watt Pottery, Crooksville, Ohio.

Reprinted from the *Crockery and Glass Journal*, March, 1961.

#505 32-ounce tea pot.

BROWN leaves form vivid motif on buff glaze in "Autumn Leaves" 8 pc. salad set, retailing for $6.98. Watt Pottery Co., Crooksville, Ohio.

Notice that this advertisment refers to "Autumn Leaves", not Autumn Foliage. Reprinted from the *Crockery and Glass Journal*, March, 1559.

Left: #115 60-ounce coffee carafe (ribbon handle). The ribbon handle carafe was apparently not sold with a lid, and are much more common than the small-handled #115 coffee server. Right: #17 ice-lip, #16, #15, #62 creamer.

#501 and #121 mugs.

The #115 carafe was sold on a candle warmer stand. Right: #110 covered baker.

#112 6-cup tea pot.

Left to right: #98 covered sugar, #62 creamer, #1219 chip-n-dip set (#119 and #120 bowls), #117 and #118 hourglass shakers (S and P holes).

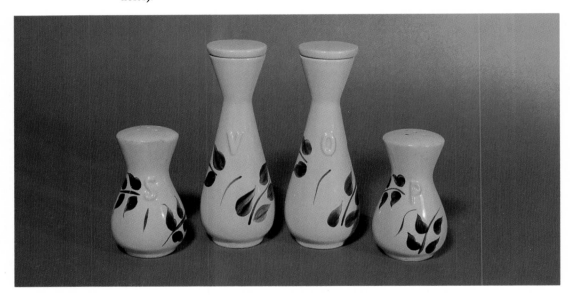

#117 and #118 hourglass shakers (raised "S" and "P"), #126 cruets.

Rear, left to right: #96 covered baker on candle warmer, #131 covered baker on #133 cut-away electric warmer. Front: #506 lug casserole and lid.

#02 stacking refrigerator set, #01 grease jar.

#59 ice bucket.

#133 non-electric base. This top of this base is flat and glazed, unike the electric base.

#106 salad bowl.

#503 and #76 cookie jars.

#31 platter.

Top to bottom: #94, #95, #96 bakers.

Ribbed nappies. #04, #05, #06, #07.

Left to right: #39 spaghetti bowl, #33 pie plate.

#73 salad bowls, inside and outside decoration.

Mixing bowls, #9 and #6.

Deep mixing bowls, #65, #64, #63.

Chapter 16
Double Apple

We don't know the introduction date of this pattern, but it is found on shapes produced between 1959 and 1962. We believe the real name of this pattern is "Crab Apple". With its brown stems and crab apple leaves, Double Apple is clearly not just a variation of the Apple pattern.

For some reason, many pieces of Double Apple have a "sandy" feeling to them, and appear to have dark specks in the glaze.

#76 bean pot/cookie jar.

#503 cookie jar.

Left to right: #62 creamer, #15 and #16 pitchers.

#96 covered baker on wire stand.

#120 dip bowl, #96 chip bowl. We have not verified this chip-n-dip combination from production records or boxed sets. Collectors have reported purchasing these sets from original owners.

#63 deep mixing bowl.

Ribbed nappies, #04, #05, #06, #07.

#73 salad bowl.

Chapter 17
Tulip

The Tulip pattern was designed much later than the Dutch Tulip. It is found on shapes from the 1960s, such as the 600 series bowls introduced in 1962. Only a small number of molds seem to have been used for Tulip. The Tulip pattern does not appear in the Watt catalogs and was sold through Woolworth stores.

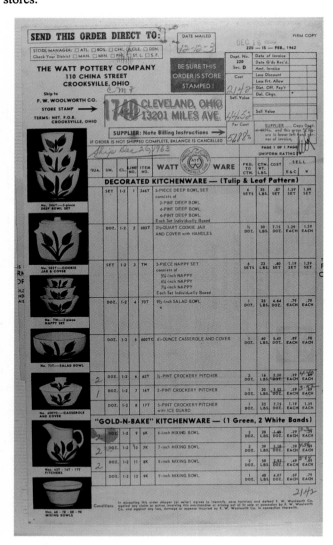

Tulip pieces could be ordered from Woolworth stores in 1963. This order form folds into a mailing envelope addressed to the Watt Pottery.

#503 cookie jar.

#39 spaghetti bowl and 5 1/2" dia, 1 3/4" h bowl with blue band.

Left to right: #65, #64, #63 deep mixing bowls.

Top to bottom: #603, #604, #600, #601 ribbed bakers.

Left to right: #601, #600 covered bakers.

#73 salad bowl.

Left to right: #62, #15, #16, #17 pitchers.

Chapter 18
Butterfly

This pattern (and its correct name) is a mystery. Interviews with former decorators from the pottery failed to turn up anyone who remembered the pattern, let alone the real name. The authors have only located a few examples, and from the shapes found so far, Butterfly could have been produced any time between 1955 and 1962.

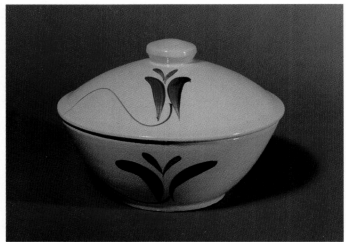

#67 covered baker.

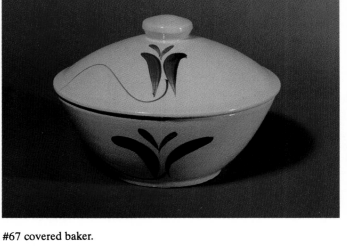

#62 creamer.

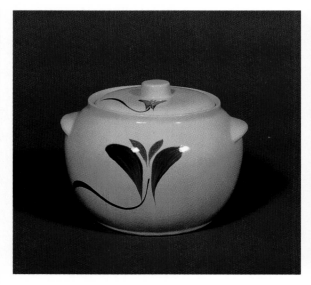

#76 cookie jar.

#16, #69 pitchers.

Chapter 19
Esmond Ware

The Watt Pottery was one of many companies who produced ware for Esmond Industries under the Esmond trade name. Some other companies were the Nelson McCoy Pottery and the Purinton Pottery. Esmond ware was also imported from Japan. Fortunately, the Watt-produced Esmond pieces are well marked and can be readily distinguished from the work of other potteries.

In March, 1957, Bennett Asquith received trademark No. 18,680 for the Esmond name written in script, for use on electrical products. He claimed use of the name since 1944. This style of the Esmond name was also featured in Esmond's advertisements for the lazy susan canisters. In 1962 Esmond Industries was located in Westbury, Long Island, with a showroom on 5th Avenue in New York City.

The most popular Esmond products among collectors today are the hand-decorated pieces with fruit designs. These designs had their beginning with the Purinton Pottery. Bernard Purinton developed the lazy susan set with the four-section canisters and wooden lid in the early 1950s. Purinton produced these sets both for themselves and for Esmond Industries. The Purinton-produced pieces may be inked-stamped on the bottom, but they are never marked in the mold.

In December, 1957, Mr. Asquith was granted design patent No. 181,776 for the "Combined Lazy Susan, Canister Set and Cover therefor". After Purinton went out of business in 1958, Esmond sought other manufacturers to produce their products. The Watt-produced Esmond ware probably dates from this period. Esmond distributed ceramic and wooden cookie jars and canisters sets through the 1980s.

Esmond ware produced by the Watt Pottery has the following distinguishing characteristics to use as guidelines:

(1) A typical Watt, deep cream colored body, not a white clay body.

(2) Watt-produced Esmond ware is always marked in the mold with a mold number and the words "ESMOND U.S.A." in all capital letters with periods in "U.S.A." Other potteries used the words "Esmond USA" with a script "E", a "fat" "M", lower case "nd" and no periods in "USA". Pieces which bear a copyright symbol marked in the mold do not appear to be Watt.

(3) Mold numbers are always marked in the mold and mold numbers specific to the Esmond line are under 100 (numbers 16, 30, 31, 32, 34, 36, 37 and 62, that we know of). Mold numbers in the 200's or 500's are not-Watt. (Of course, regular production Watt molds with Esmond decorations, such as a #17 pitcher, will have typical Watt bottom marks.)

(4) In the fruit patterns, the leaves are typical Watt green, not blue-green. The Watt grape bunch has two leaves, most other potteries used six leaves

(5) Brown/black shaded ware was produced by Watt and McCoy. Look for good bottom marks.

(6) None of the ware with the "orange ripple" glaze (or other different colored ripple glazes) is Watt. Pieces with this glaze all appear to have been made by the Nelson McCoy Pottery.

We have included ware with a single band of sprayed, brown glaze in this chapter. Although we have not found this decoration on Esmond molds, it is similar to the brown/black shaded Esmond decoration.

#17 ice-lip pitcher and #31 mug in Esmond apple.

Beautiful 15" wooden carousel with candle warmer stand for the central #76 bean pot decorated with Esmond apple and pear. Eight #75 bean cups with Esmond apples fit around the edge.

#17 ice-lip picher with Esmond grape pattern, surrounded by #31 mugs with Esmond apples.

#31 mugs in Esmond pineapple and grape.

Cookie jars in apple and pear pattern. Left to right: Esmond #36, 10" dia, 7 1/2" h w/lid; Esmond #34, 8 1/2" dia, 8" h w/lid.

Lazy susans, each piece has a different Esmond fruit on it. Left to right: #62 barrel-shaped, 11" dia, 10 1/2" h; #32, 10 1/4" dia, 10 1/2" h.

Left to right: #73 salad bowl, #31 platter, Esmond #37 casserole (8 1/2" dia, 5" h w/lid), all in Esmond apple and pear.

One piece of a #30 square canister set. 7" h without lid.

Rear, left to right: Esmond #37 casserole, Esmond #36 cookie jar. Front: #75 bean cups, all in black/brown shaded.

Deep mixing bowls in fruit patterns. Left to right: #65, #64, #63.

Esmond #34 Happy/Sad cookie jar.

Reverse of Happy/Sad cookie jar.

Left to right: bowl, 5 1/2" dia, 2"h; Esmond #16 casserole, 4" dia, 3" h w/lid.

Front to rear: Esmond #16 casserole, Esmond #34 cookie jar, #31 platter, all in black/brown shaded.

#17 ice-lip pitcher and #31 mugs in black/brown shaded.

#61 mug in black/brown shaded.

#17 ice-lip pitcher, #31 mug, #701 mug, all in black/brown shaded.

#62 creamer in brown-spray bands.

#17 ice-lip pitcher and #701 mugs in brown-spray bands.

#32 canister set in black/brown shaded.

Comparison between Watt and not-Watt Esmond canisters. The Watt pieces are on the left. Notice the typical Watt cream color clay, and green/dark green leaves. The not-Watt pieces on the right are too white, and the leaves are two-tone green and blue-green.

Comparison of bottom marks. Watt pieces (on the left) always have large, all-capital letter ESMOND marks, and mold numbers under 100. This particular not-Watt piece on the right has no bottom marks. Not-Watt pieces also tend to have distinct mold lines on the bottom.

NOT-WATT. Esmond marks like this, with a script "E", a fat "M", lower-case "nd", and mold numbers in the 200s are never Watt.

NOT-WATT. We have found no Esmond pieces in these orange and blue ripple glazes which we would attribute to Watt. This appears to be a glaze unique to the Nelson McCoy Pottery. The small casserole is marked #216, it is the same mold as the Watt-produced #16 casserole. The pitchers are #220. There is also a yellow variation of these glazes.

Chapter 20
Stenciled Ware

This ware was produced by spraying thinned colored slip through a stencil, using an air-powered spray gun. They are not free-hand decorated pieces. Eagle is the only actual pattern produced this way.

EAGLE

Left to right: Eagle #17 ice-lip pitcher, #72 tapered cookie jar, #601 covered baker.

Eagle #59 ice bucket.

Left to right: Eagle #76 cookie jar, #601 covered baker.

Eagle ribbed mixing bowls, 9", 8", 7", 5".

MISCELLANEOUS

Goodies jars, left to right: #59, #72, #76. The #59 Goodies jar has a different lid than the normal ice bucket.

Reprinted from the *Crockery and Glass Journal*, July, 1952.

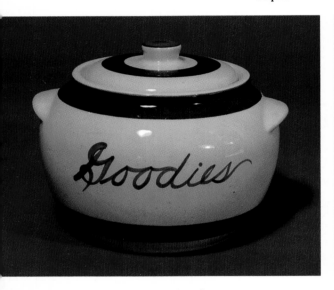

#76 Goodies jar with script lettering.

Mexican motif bowls with brown spray bands. Left: #603's. Right: #601. These bowls were made for the Texas Chili Company.

Snack set, top to bottom: #4, #52, #7, #54.

On the left is a Watt #603 Mexican motif bowl, on the right is an Ath-Tex bowl which is not-Watt. Notice the ragged edges of the sprayed band, an Ath-Tex characteristic. There are also bowls with Mexican motif imported from Japan.

136 Stenciled Ware

Chapter 21
Corn Row

This embossed ware was produced beginning in 1952. The real name is not known. The advertisements called it "Rainbow", but seemed to refer more to the colors than to the design. Hazel Watt (Mrs. W.I. Watt) was known to call it "Corn Row," and that is the name we have chosen to use. It is possible to assemble a collection all in blue, silver and rose, which makes for a very different color combination.

#15 pitcher, clear glaze, with advertising.

#17, #16 and #15 pitchers in blue, silver and rose.

#21 cookie jars in rose and silver.

Aqua casserole, 8 1/2" dia, 4 1/2" h w/lid.

Mixing bowls: #6 yellow, #7 brown, #8 silver, #9 blue.

#8 blue nappy, rose custard cup 3 1/4" dia, 2 1/4" h.

Chapter 22
Kolor Kraft

Kolor-Kraft was introduced in January, 1954. At first glance, this embossed pattern might seem identical to Swirl from the 1940s. There are basic differences, however, and no molds are the same. The ribs on the earlier Swirl pieces are recurved. (See Chapter 5) The outer lips of bowls in the two patterns are different. Kolor-Kraft can be found with a lip and long shoulder combination, or just a shoulder with no lip.

The Brush Pottery used the name, "Kolorkraft" around 1930. Their kitchen ware line had vertical embossed ribs in solid color glazes, similar to the Watt Pottery's Corn Row pattern.

#21 cookie jar, #56 tumbler.

Covered bakers, #54 gray, #53 rose.

#17 green, #16 brown, #15 yellow pitchers.

Mixing bowl set with lip and shoulder. #5 through #9.

Mixing bowl set with shoulder only, no lip. #5 through #9. Colors in
this style bowls are more subtle.

#9 covered bowl, green.

#7 bowl, no lip, with brown bands on the shoulder.

Yellow #52 baker, green #4 mixing bowl. NOTE: we believe this
small bowl was part of a salesman's sample kit. It is not a Watt
production bowl size.

Chapter 23
Basket Weave

Basket Weave pieces are produced in three different numbered series. The pieces sold through the Watt Pottery are numbered from #99 through #127. These are different molds than the Orchard Ware pieces with the same number range.

Pieces marked "Heirloom" were produced by Watt and marketed through the Salem China Company of Salem, Ohio. The Heirloom name is registered to them. Heirloom ware is marked with a picture of a castle on the larger pieces (see Chapter 32 for bottom marks). The main colors of Heirloom are a high-gloss brown, and a dark mustard color. A few pieces were made in other colors. Mold numbers range from #801 through #816. Many of the shapes are unique to Heirloom, while others (such as the pitchers) are Watt shapes.

J.C. Stoneware is a name which we have not yet fully traced. Interviews with Watt employees revealed that it was produced for a St. Louis supermarket chain, but we have not discovered which one. Most shapes are the same as Heirloom, but although the mold numbers are also in the 800s, they are different than the Heirloom numbers for the same piece. The J.C. Stoneware brown glaze is Watt brown, not Heirloom gloss brown.

WATT BASKET WEAVE

#101 cookie jars, blue and yellow. # 101 jars came with white lids.
7 1/4" dia, 6" h, 6 3/4" h w/lid

Assortment of #100 salad bowls, 10" dia, 4" h; and #102 individual
bowls, 5 1/2" dia, 2" h.

Green and pink #101 cookie jars.

#99 covered baker, 7 1/2" dia, 3 1/4" h, 4 1/4" h w/lid.

Boxed salad set, #100 salad bowl and #102 individual bowls, plus fork and spoon.

#127 stacking refrigerator jars, assorted colors, 4 1/2" dia, 3" h, 3 1/4" h w/lid.

Basket Weave plates. Left, front to rear: 6 1/2" aqua saucer, 7 1/2" plate in gloss brown, 9 1/2" plate, mustard. Right, front to rear: 6 1/2" medium brown saucer, 7 1/2" ivory plate, 9 1/2" gloss brown plate.

HEIRLOOM   Basket Weave mixing bowls, 5" through 9".

Heirloom #810 pitchers, (same size as Watt #17) in gloss brown and mustard.

Left to right: Heirloom gloss brown #806 mug (3 1/2" dia, 5 1/2" h),
J.C. Stoneware medium brown #801 mug (same as Watt #121),
Heirloom gloss brown #801 mug (same as Watt #701), Heirloom
mustard #806 mug.

J.C. STONEWARES

Heirloom #812 bean pots in gloss brown, and mustard w/medium brown lid (they seem to be found this way), #816 bean cups, gloss brown and mustard.

Left to right: J.C. Stoneware #806 yellow salad bowl, Watt #100 brown individual bowls and Watt #102 peach salad bowl.

Left to right: J.C. Stoneware #800 cookie jar in medium brown, Heirloom #811 cookie jar in gloss brown. 7 1/2" dia, 7" h, 9" h w/lid.

Heirloom #803 salad bowl, 10" dia, 4" h; and #807 individual bowls, gloss brown.

Left to right: Heirloom #815 lug casserole, 8" dia, 3 1/2" h; 6" h w/lid in mustard with mismatched medium brown lid, Heirloom #814 gloss brown individual lug 4 3/4" dia, 2" h; Heirloom #815 gloss brown.

Left to right: J.C. Stoneware #803 medium brown casserole, Heirloom #802 gloss brown casserole. 9" dia, 3 1/2" h, 6 1/2" h w/lid.

Left to right: J.C. Stoneware medium brown #805 baker, 8 1/4" dia, 3 1/2" h; Heirloom #808 (same as Watt #99).

#803 J. C. Stoneware casserole and #808 mug, medium brown.

Left to right: Heirloom #802, 9" dia, 3 1/2" h, 6 1/2" h w/lid; in cream with mismatched medium brown lid, Heirloom #808.

Heirloom mixing bowls, #803 (6"), #804 (7"), #805 (8") in gloss brown and mustard.

Chapter 24
Wood Grain

The Wood Grain dinnerware line was made in two different styles by Watt. The first pieces made were a series produced for the Robert B. Owens & Associates of Chicago (apparently no relation to any of the Owens potteries) in 1958. The wood graining on these pieces is somewhat stylized, made up of nearly straight lines and round "knots." The Watt Wood Grain is more like the grain in real wood.

The Owens pieces are numbered from #200 through #208, although the mixing bowls are marked like standard Watt mixing bowls, #5 through #9. Owens pieces have been found with either a "Watt" bottom mark, or an "Owens Ceramic" mark (see Chapter 32 for bottom marks).

The Watt Wood Grain series features a graining pattern that is much different from the Owens ware. They are marked from #605W through #627W.

Wood Grain pieces marked "Ath-Tex", or unmarked on the bottom, are *not Watt*. They are produced by the Ath-Tex Pottery of Athens, Texas. This company was founded by Charles Norman and Watt Norman, cousins of W.I. Watt. It appears that Ath-Tex acquired some of the Watt molds, as some shapes are identical to Watt pieces. All Watt Wood Grain pieces are clearly marked in the mold. Ath-Tex pieces can further be distinguished by the smeared appearance of the over-glaze. Watt pieces are cleanly wiped.

OWENS WOOD GRAIN

Owens canisters with dome lids, butterscotch glaze with white interior, left to right: #201 "Flour" w/lid, 7 1/4" dia, 7" h, 8 3/4" h; #202 "Sugar" canister, 6" dia, 6" h; #203 "Coffee" canister w/lid, 5" dia, 5" h, 6 1/2" h. "Tea" canister is missing.

OWENS CERAMICS

New "Streamliner" Profit Line – Only Big Selling Casual & Ovenware Pieces

- Selected Items For Fast Turnover
- Limited Colors for Low Inventory
- Low, Low Prices For Volume Sales
- Quality-controlled for Customer Satisfaction

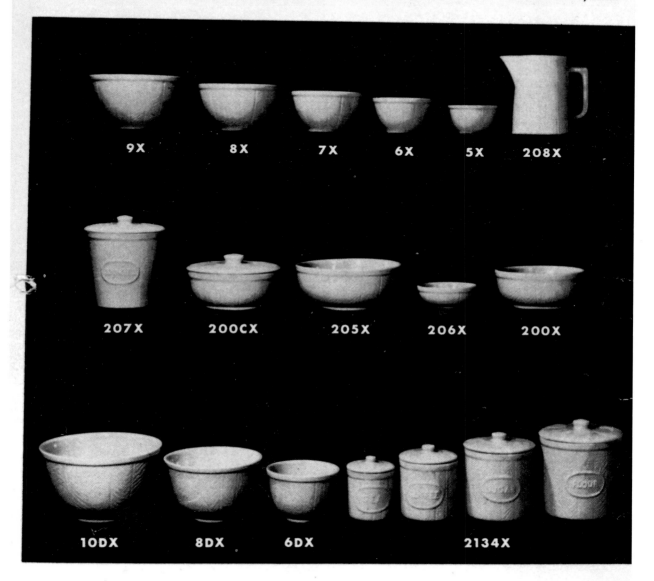

Mixing Bowls • 5 Pint Pitcher • Covered Casserole • Covered Cookie Jar

Salad Bowls and Salad Set • Special Deep Bowl Set • 8 Piece Canister Set

Sales: Robert B. Owens & Associates, Inc., 28 E. Jackson Blvd. Chicago 4, Ill. (WA 2-1929)

Manufacture and Billing: OWENS CERAMICS, P. O. Box 31, Crooksville, Ohio

1958 flyer from Owens Ceramic for Watt-produced ware.

Owens canisters with flat lids, russet glaze with white interior, left to right: #202 "Sugar" canister, 6" dia, 6" h, 7" h w/lid; #204 "Tea" canister, 4" dia, 4 1/4" h, 5" h w/lid. "Flour" and "Coffee" canisters missing.

Owens mixing bowls, 5", 6", and 7" in green, 9" in yellow.

Owens #202 "Sugar" canister in green glaze.

Owens #207 cookie jar, wiped brown glaze. 7" dia, 6 3/4" h, 7 3/4" h w/lid.

Owens #205 baker in yellow, 10" dia, 4" h.

Owens #8D deep mixing bowl, green.

Left: Watt #608C in wiped brown, 9" dia, 4 1/4" h, 6" h w/lid. Right: Owens #200C in yellow, 8 1/2" dia, 3 1/2" h, 4 1/2" h w/lid.

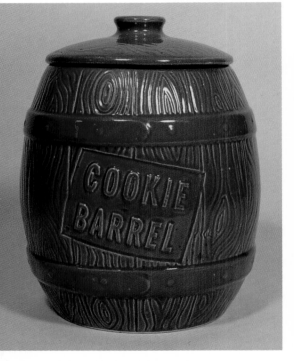

#617W cookie barrel, later style, russet glaze. 6" top dia, 10 1/2" h.

Wiped brown cookie barrels. Left: #617W from 1963, with bands overlapping from right side. (Note that brown glaze is smeared, and this style of cookie barrel is frequently found with a crude bottom, both of which could indicate that some were made by another manufacturer.) Right: #617W from 1964 with bands overlapping from the left side. Note the differences in the wood grain figures in these two barrels. Obviously there were two separate molds.

#618W bean pots, wiped brown and russet. 6 1/2" top dia, 7 1/2" h.

Wood Grain pitchers, wiped brown. Left to right: #615W (9" h),
#614W (7 1/2" h), #613W (5 3/4" h).

Russet Wood Grain bowls. Left to right: #610W, #605W, #608C.

#626W and #627W Wood Grain shakers in russet glaze.

#613W and #614W pitchers, russet.

#612W bowls in brown spray band, and wiped brown, 5 1/2" dia, 2" h.

Wiped brown Wood Grain mixing bowls. Top to bottom: #606W (6 1/2" dia), #607W (7 1/2" dia), #608W (8 1/2" dia), #610W (10" dia). There is also a #605W bowl.

NOT-WATT! This is an Ath-Tex bottom mark. Some Ath-Tex pieces are not marked, but all Watt Wood Grain is marked Watt and has a 600W series number.

NOT-WATT! These Ath-Tex pieces and others are not products of the Watt Pottery. They can be told by the smeared overglaze and different bottom marks. The pitchers do not have dark brown handles like the Watt Wood Grain pitchers.

Comparison between a Watt #611W bowl (right), and an Ath-Tex bowl (left) made from the same mold. Note the smeared overglaze on the Ath-Tex bowl and the lack of a Watt bottom mark and 600W series number.

ICED TEA KEGS

The iced tea kegs are the oldest Watt products in continuous production. They appear in the 1940 production records, and were sold throughout the Pottery's existence. At first they were only marked, "Iced Tea". In the 1950s, trade names were made available to customers. More than 40 different trade names have been identified so far.

Iced tea kegs were formed by jiggering and were the largest pieces of Watt ware produced since the stoneware production ceased in 1935. Different molds were not required for each trade name. Each name was fashioned onto a wooden plug which could be inserted into the mold for the keg. In this fashion, even a small number of kegs could be made for a customer once the plug was made.

Kegs marked "Iced Tea" or "Iced Coffee" are part #400, while "Lemonade" kegs are part #401. This is followed by the number of gallons (#400-3, #401-2). The kegs are not commonly marked with the mold number (see Chapter 32 for bottom marks). The kegs were made in three sizes, but only one size, the two-gallon keg, is common. Three gallon kegs have been found, but the one gallon keg mentioned in production records has yet to be found by the authors.

Sizes vary somewhat from keg to keg, but a two-gallon keg measures approximately 11" tall without lid and is about 29" in circumference around the middle. A three-gallon keg is 12" tall and about 32 1/2" around. They appear to use the same lid.

Brown "Tartan" and aqua "Iced Nestea."

Comparison between a #400-2, two-gallon keg on the left and a #400-3, three-gallon keg on the right.

Golden brown "Iced Tea" and gloss brown "Fleetwood."

Golden "Ireland" and brown "Rotary Coffee Co."

Brown "5th Ave" and russet "Stewart's."

Gloss brown "Grants" and yellow #401-2 "Lemonade."

Russet "Old Reliable" and brown "Breakfast Cheer."

Brown "Our Seal" and russet "L.H. Parke Co."

Brown "Refreshing Iced Coffee" and russet "Maxwell House."

Russet "Tetley" and brown "Ko-We-Ba."

Golden "Cambridge" and ivory "Salada."

Russet "Quinn's" and brown with red lettering "Quinn's."

Russet "Superior" and golden "Douglas."

Russet "National Coffee" and golden "Continental Coffee Company."

Brown "Goodrich" and russet "Van Roy."

Brown with brown letters "Bernice" and green "Parkway, C.D. Kenny Co."

Brown "Stanley Brothers" and aqua "Iced Tea."

Chapter 25
Kathy Kale

The Kathy Kale trade name, Royal Danish pattern, is the last new line of ware which the Watt Pottery was producing when the fire of 1965 ended production. Only about four car loads were shipped. Royal Danish ware was destined for the Kroger Company, with initial distribution in the St. Louis district of 25 stores. The contract was a large one, expected to increase annual sales by one third.

The authors have not been able to trace the origin of the Kathy Kale name. Ware with this trade name was produced by the Watt, Nelson McCoy, and Canonsburg Potteries. *Very little ware marked Kathy Kale was produced by Watt.* The most commonly found Kathy Kale ware was produced by McCoy. There are two McCoy patterns: one with a hand-decorated apple design, and the other in a brown glaze with a white flow over the top edge. (Photos of both are shown for comparison.) We have not identified Canonsburg's Kathy Kale line.

While the Watt Kathy Kale may be hard to find, it is distinctive. All pieces feature a deeply embossed pattern in a basket weave or "Roman key" design. The saucers have no embossing. Production colors are white, with saucers and lids of covered pieces in blue. Several pieces were photographed in other colors. It is not known if they were intended to be production colors. Glaze sample pieces have survived, however, and they have the test glaze number incised on the bottom.

Congratulations! for having chosen

ROYAL DANISH
STONEWARE

The charm of this lovely Scandinavian-styled pottery lies not only on its sculptured design . . . but in the mark of distinction it carries as fine-quality "handcrafted" stoneware.

For you will notice as your set grows, that no two pieces are exactly alike in size, coloring or glaze. In a time when modern machines can produce hundreds and thousands of "like" objects a minute—the age-old technique of creating this beautiful hand-crafted stoneware gives "Royal Danish" dinnerware a matchless charm and quality!

Highly skilled people, trained in the fine art of pottery making, watch over each step of the long, slow process it takes to produce this fine quality stoneware. After each piece is carefully shaped and embossed with this weave-

like Danish-inspired pattern—it is fired at very high temperatures for many hours in gas fired kilns. This gives the ware its tough glossy finish that is impervious to oven heat or strong detergents. (A kiln is similar to your own gas oven, but is able to get many times as hot).

Stacked on special cars, the Stoneware takes a long 24-hour journey through the kiln. Where it is stacked, on the top, to the side, on the bottom, determines its eventual coloring and shape. (As with your own oven—the heat intensifies near the top, and results in a shade darker coloring, and a slight more shrink in the pottery).

The end result?

RICH, HIGHLY GLOSSED DINNERWARE THAT YOU CAN BAKE IN, SERVE IN . . . AND TAKE PRIDE IN — Royal Danish Stoneware!

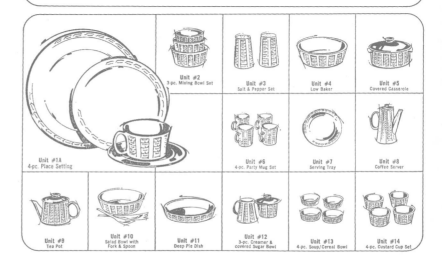

Unit #2 — 3-pc. Mixing Bowl Set
Unit #3 — Salt & Pepper Set
Unit #4 — Low Baker
Unit #5 — Covered Casserole
Unit #1A — 4-pc. Place Setting
Unit #6 — 4-pc. Party Mug Set
Unit #7 — Serving Tray
Unit #8 — Coffee Server
Unit #9 — Tea Pot
Unit #10 — Salad Bowl with Fork & Spoon
Unit #11 — Deep Pie Dish
Unit #12 — 3-pc. Creamer & covered Sugar Bowl
Unit #13 — 4-pc. Soup/Cereal Bowl
Unit #14 — 4-pc. Custard Cup Set

Brochure packed with each Royal Danish purchase.

Royal Danish ware was tested in many glazes before selecting the production colors. 8" luncheon plates, cups and saucers.

Tea pot and coffee server in chartreuse glaze.

Tea pot, 4 1/2" dia, 5 1/2" h.

Coffee server, 10 1/2" h.

10 1/2" dinner plate, cup and saucer.

14" platter and deep pie dish, 9" dia, 2" h.

Royal Danish mixing bowls, 6 1/2" dia, 2 1/2" h, and 8 1/4" dia, 4" h.

Salt and pepper shakers, sugar and covered sugar bowl, all 4 1/2" h.

Casseroles with green and blue lids, 7 1/2" dia, 5" h w/lid.

Royal Danish ware came sealed in plastic like these custard cups, 4" dia, 2 3/4" h.

Royal Danish salad set. Salad bowl, 11" dia, 2 1/2" h; and individual salad bowls, 5 1/2" dia, 2" h.

Coffee cup, 4" dia, 2 1/2" h; and party mug, 4" dia, 5" h.

NOT-WATT! None of the Kathy Kale ware in this gloss brown glaze with cream drip was made by Watt. Most pieces seem to be McCoy molds, some may have been produced by the Canonsburg Pottery as well.

NOT-WATT! All Kathy Kale ware in this apple design was produced by the Nelson McCoy Pottery and sold under their Kitchen Accessories line.

Chapter 26
Orchard Ware

Orchard Ware means two different things in regards to the Watt Pottery. It is both a shape name and a pattern name (actually a series of color combinations). Orchard Ware is a trade name used by Newland, Schneeloch and Piek (NS&P) of New York, from as early as the 1930s until recently. Over the years their ware was produced by many china, pottery and glass companies. Other, similar names which NS&P also used are "Orchard Crystal" and "Orchard D'Ware." Orchard Ware bottom marks used by companies other than Watt are very different, primarily paper labels.

As marked on the bottom of the Watt pieces, Orchard Ware is a *shape* name, and is marked on mold numbers from #106 through #132. Most of these pieces were designed by Eva Zeisel in 1954, and the rest were added to compliment the line. These shapes appeared in the Watt catalog in 1959.

As a *pattern* name, we use Orchard Ware to mean the various two-tone dripped and spattered glaze combinations. This chapter features these Orchard Ware *patterns*. This Watt ware was sold through NS&P beginning in the early 1950s, thus the Orchard Ware connection. Two of the earliest color combinations were Black Beauty and Greenbriar. These early Orchard Ware patterns are found on standard Watt shapes.

In 1959, Watt introduced the Orchard Ware series of molds, i.e. the Orchard Ware *shapes*. New color combinations such as Nassau (cinnamon specks on clear glaze) were created for the new ware, and are found only on Orchard Ware shapes. The new shapes were very pleasing and modern, and were produced with hand-decorated patterns as well. Autumn Foliage, introduced in 1959, is commonly found on the Orchard Ware shapes. Appar-

ently, Orchard Ware shapes with the Watt hand-decorated patterns were sold by Watt, not NS&P.

The combination of a brown glaze with a contrasting white drip over the top edge was one of the most common Orchard Ware patterns. It was affectionately known as "Brown Betty" to Watt employees. This glaze combination has been produced by many other potteries, especially the Hull and Nelson McCoy Potteries. It appears that the Watt pottery was the first to use this glaze combination. It was one of Watt's supermarket lines.

We have identified the following Orchard Ware color combinations (names are given if known):

> Brown with white drip
> Brown with cream drip
> Brown with olive drip
> Brown with cinnamon drip
> Black with white drip (Black Beauty)
> Green with white drip
> Aqua with white drip (Greenbriar)
> Cream with brown drip
> Yellow with brown drip (Westwood)
> Yellow with green drip
> Blue with cobalt drip
> Pink with white drip
> Light blue with white drip
> Teal with black drip
> Cream with cinnamon specks (Nassau)
> Pink with black specks.
> Pink with large black spots
> Pink with white loops

Brown/white drip pitchers, left to right:
#62, #15, #16.

A #69 refrigerator pitcher in brown/white drip.

#62 creamers in brown/white drip and brown/cinnamon drip.

#132 carafes in brown/cinnamon drip and brown/olive drip (lid missing).

Left to right: #15 brown/olive drip, #16 brown/cinnamon, #16 and #15, brown/cream drip.

Rear, left to right: # 60 bowl, #61 mug, #18 tab handled casserole.
Front: #101 plate, all in brown/white drip.

#121 mug, brown/cinnamon drip.

#59 ice bucket in metal holder, brown/white drip.

#84 square casserole in metal candle warmer stand, brown/white drip.

Left: #130 tureen, brown/olive drip. Right: #131 covered bowl in brown/olive drip on a #133 electric warmer with solid base.

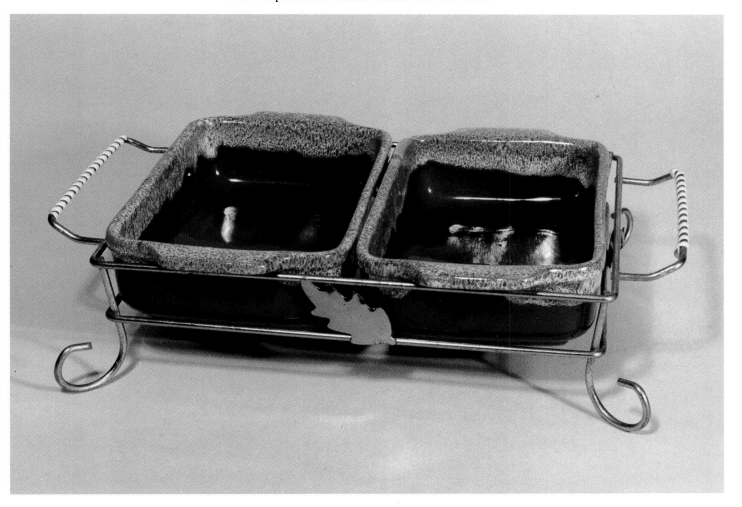

Stands were available to hold a pair of #85 rectangular bakers. Brown/white drip.

#96 covered bakers, brown with cream and cinnamon drip.

#130 tureen with slotted lid in brown/olive drip, on a #133 electric warmer with cut-away base.

#1219 chip-n-dip set. #119 and #120 bowls in brown/cinnamon drip.

#506 covered casserole, brown/white drip.

#54 covered baker, brown/white drip.

#58 fruit bowl, brown/white drip.

Left, top: #74, bottom: #60. Right: #18 French handled casserole, all in brown/white drip.

#73 salad bowl and #74 individual salad bowls, brown/white drip.

Deep mixing bowl set, #65, #64, #63 in brown/white drip.

#59 ice bucket, Black Beauty.

Black Beauty beverage set pictured in advertisement, #17 plain-lip pitcher and #56 straight side tumblers.

Black Beauty salad set, #55 salad bowl, #52 individual salad bowls.

#54 covered baker on candle warmer stand, Black Beauty.

Left to right: #54 covered baker, #49 grease jar, #53 covered baker,
all in Black Beauty.

NEW PRODUCTS: PITTSBURGH SHOWS

Black Beauty: rich-looking earthenware beverage set, black with speckled white overglaze trim. Suitable for use indoors or out. Seven pieces retail for $3.95. Available from Newland, Schneeloch & Piek, 1107 Broadway, N.Y.C.

Reprinted from the *Crockery and Glass Journal*, February, 1953.

#58 fruit bowl in Black Beauty.

Nine piece Black Beauty or Greenbriar salad set, with white drip glaze, is also ovenproof; sells for $4.98. Large mixing bowl is 11½" in diameter; small bowls are 6". Newland, Schneeloch & Piek, 1107 Broadway, NYC.

Reprinted from the *Crockery and Glass Journal*, June, 1952.

#45 and #46 barrel shakers, Greenbriar.

Greenbriar salad set pictured in advertisement, #55 salad bowl, #52 individual salad bowls.

Greenbriar casseroles, #54 and #18 grooved handle.

#39 spaghetti bowl, Greenbriar.

#17 plain-lip pitcher and #56 straight side tumbler, Greenbriar.

Greenbriar 10" mixing bowl.

#55 salad bowl and #75 bean cups, Greenbriar.

The Nassau combination salad set. #117 and #118 shakers, #126 cruets, #106 salad bowl and plastic fork and spoon. The small #120 bowl enables use as a chip-n-dip, also. The metal holder has a "shelf" to support the small bowl, with a hoop 4 1/2" inside diameter. This set uses only Orchard Ware (shape) pieces.

Nassau salad set, #106 salad bowls, and #120 individual salad bowls. These #120 bowls are *salad* bowls, not dip bowls. They have a plain base, not a stepped base.

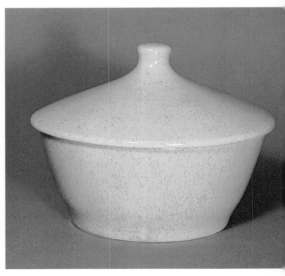

#110 casserole, Nassau.

#15 and #16 pitchers, green/white drip.

Light blue/white drip berry/salad set. #58 fruit bowl, #60 individual
bowls on metal ring.

#115 ribbon handle carafe, blue/cobalt drip on candle warmer stand.

#115 ribbon handle carafe, teal/black drip.

#117 and #118 shakers, blue/cobalt drip.

#31 platter and 10" plate, teal/black drip.

Pink/white drip salad set. #73 salad bowl, #74 individual bowls.

#58 bowl in pink with white icing.

#54 covered baker on candle warmer stand, pink/black specks.

#58 fruit bowl, pink/black specks.

#58 fruit bowl, pink/black spots.

#59 ice bucket, pink/black specks.

#59 ice bucket, pink/black spots (no lid).

#60 bowl, pink/black spots.

Cream/brown drip #16 pitcher.

#96 covered baker, Westwood.

Cream/brown drip #59 ice bucket.

#1219 chip-n-dip set, #119 and #120 bowls, Westwood.

#89 "canoe" bowl, cream/brown drip (this is a large bowl, 11" long).

#88 individual "canoe" bowl, 6 1/2" long, cream/brown drip.

Left to right: #54 covered baker and #86 oval casserole, cream/brown drip.

Chapter 27
Banded Ware

Banded ware has been produced by the Watt Pottery since about 1935. The ware in this chapter is modern banded ware, from the 1950s and 60s. Only two color combinations have pattern names, Kitch-N-Queen (blue/rose bands) and Par-T-Que (three brown bands). The Gold-N-Bake name was used for ware with blue/white bands and green/white bands, but was also found marked on ware with hand-decorated patterns.

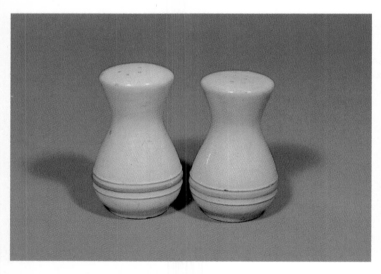

#117 and #118 Kitch-N-Queen hourglass shakers.

Kitch-N-Queen #67 covered baker.

Kitch-N-Queen covered bakers. Left to right: #600, #110, #601.

Kitch-N-Queen mixing bowls come in more sizes than any other Watt pattern. Top to bottom: #5, #6, #7, #8, #9, #10, #12, #14, #616 (16" bowl).

Kitch-N-Queen #17 ice-lip pitcher.

#01 Kitch-N-Queen grease jar.

#59 Kitch-N-Queen ice bucket.

Ribbed Kitch-N-Queen mixing bowls, #5 through #9.

Kitch-N-Queen cookie jars, #503 and #76.

Kitch-N-Queen ribbed bakers. Rear, left to right: #601, #600, #604.
Front, left to right: #602, #603.

Kitch-N-Queen deep mixing bowls. Left to right: #65, #64, #63.

An assortment of Kitch-N-Queen bowls. Left to right: #73 salad
bowl, #67 baker, #05 nappy.

Kitch-N-Queen #33 pie plate.

Par-T-Que hourglass shakers, #117 and #118.

Watt called the brown-banded ware, "Par-T-Que", or "Bar-B-Q". This ware has thin, brush-decorated bands, not the heavy bands of other banded ware. Reprinted from the *Crockery and Glass Journal*, December, 1959.

Par-T-Que #17 ice-lip pitcher, #62 creamer and #98 covered sugar.

Par-T-Que tea set. Rear, left to right: #112 6-cup tea pot, #115 60-ounce coffee server (small handle). #121 mugs on #31 platter.

Par-T-Que #121 mugs were also made with advertising. Notice that the bands are moved down to make room for the lettering.

#01 grease jar, Par-T-Que.

Par-T-Que #503 cookie jar.

Par-T-Que #64 deep mixing bowl (part of 63, 64, 65 set).

Par-T-Que tableware. Rear, left to right: #101 dinner plate, #31
platter, #102 luncheon plate. Front: #44 flat soup bowl.

Watt banded pie plates come in all colors.

Potpourri of mixing bowls. #6 black band, #7 brown band, #8 blue/
white band, #12 green/white band.

These #39 spaghetti bowls in blue or red bands are very colorful
blended in with patterned ware.

Green and white banded ware was
marketed as the Gold-N-Bake line. #5
through #9 ribbed mixing bowls.

Blue/white banded ware. Rear, left to right: old style pitcher, #17 plain-lip pither. Front: the blue banded #75 bean cups marked: "Penna. Dutch Days, Hershey, PA.", are very collectible.

#59 ice bucket, green/white bands.

Blue/white banded #54 covered baker.

#5 through #9 blue/white mixing bowls, 8" old style baker, marked "Gold-N-Bake".

#53 covered baker, brown bands. NOTE: these are heavy, slip bands, not the thin, brushed bands of Par-T-Que.

Black banded #73 salad bowl.

Black banded #6, #7, #8 mixing bowls.

Chapter 28
Solid Color Ware

A relatively small number of Watt molds have been found glazed in solid colors. Some patterns, like Brownstone, use two colors of glaze, but they are not dripped or spattered together like the Orchard Ware glazes. The most common Watt solid color pieces are the bean pots and bean cups in brown glaze. This color was called "French Crust Brown."

These #29, 10" dinner plates could be Past-L or Gala-Color dinnerware, listed by Watt in the 1940s, but not identified yet.

BROWNSTONE

Brownstone-green pichers, #15, #16, #17 ice-lip.

Brownstone-green range set. #117 and #118 hourglass shakers, #01 grease jar.

Brownstone-green ribbed bakers. Left to right: #604, #602.

Brownstone-green ribbed mixing bowls, #6 through #9.

Difference between Brownstone-green and blue: Brownstone-green has brown lids, and Brownstone-blue has blue lids. #601 green, and #600 blue, covered bakers.

Brownstone-blue #17 ice-lip pitcher, #121 mug and #62 creamer.

Brownstone-blue #117 and #118 hourglass shakers.

Brownstone-blue #76 bean pot.

Brownstone-blue #75 bean cups and #96 baker.

BISQUE

Bisque shakers and cruets. Left to right: #117 and #118 hourglass shakers (raised "S" and "P"), #126 cruets, #117 and #118 shakers ("S" and "P" holes).

Bisque #1219 chip-n-dip set with #119 and #120 bowls.

Bisque salad set: #73 salad bowl, #74 individual salad bowls.

Much of the Watt bisque ware was distributed by the Ben S. Loeb
Company under the "Joan of Arc" trade name.

BRONZE LUSTER

Bronze luster ware was distributed through the Lazarus chain of stores. It was removed from sale immediately because of high lead content. Rear, left to right: deep mixing bowls #65, #64, #63. Front: #117 amd #118 hourglass shakers, #15 pitcher.

#49, 12" chop plate, bronze luster.

Bronze luster #601 covered baker.

#115 60-ounce carafe with no handle or spout in bronze luster glaze. This is the way Eva Zeisel designed the carafe in 1954.

A trio of #4 bowls in black glaze adorn this unique lazy susan. The finial is silver plated. 8 1/2" h.

Three #115 carafes. Left to right: teal glaze (small handle), teal/black drip (ribbon handle), black (small handle).

Yellow #115 60-ounce carafe, small handle.

#69 refrigerator pitcher, brown glaze.

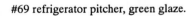

#69 refrigerator pitcher, green glaze.

#501 mugs. Watt produced some ware in clear glaze, with and without advertising. We have seen mugs, pitchers, and cookie jars.

Front, left to right: #101 dinner plate, #102 luncheon plate. Rear: #75
bean cups, brown glaze.

#75 8-ounce bean cups with stacking lid, #77 16-ounce bean cup.
There is a stacking lid for the #77, also.

Brown bean pots, left to right: #502 (4 quart), #76 (2 1/2 quart), #93
(1 1/2 quart).

Unusual #89 "canoe" bowl, 11" l, 9" w, 4" h. There is a smaller #88 "canoe" bowl also.

#76 bean pot with Campbell's Kids embossed in bisque.

Yellow custard cup, 3 1/2" dia, 2 1/2" h.

#75 yellow bean cup.

Watt produced ribbed mixing bowls in solid and two-tone combinations. This #9 bowl is suntan outside and yellow inside.

Chapter 29
Limited Production Ware

COOKIE JARS

We have included in this chapter those cookie jars which do not belong with the standard cookie jars (#21, #76, #503, etc.) produced in the hand decorated patterns. Other local potteries, such as the Nelson McCoy Pottery, produced extensive lines of cookie jars. The Watt Pottery produced only a few different cookie jars, and all of them in this chapter are scarce today.

The Policeman cookie jar was introduced at the January, 1951, Pittsburg Pottery and Glass Exhibit. The fire later that month probably destroyed the mold and only a small number of Policemen were made. Originally it was thought that only 12 were made. Talks with pottery employees revealed that the seconds were decorated and sold also. The bottom is a #59 ice bucket mold. 7 1/2" dia, 10 1/2" h.

This advertisement indicated that the Policeman could be purchased in several colors. Only the black-trimmed version has been found to date.Reprinted from the *Crockery and Glass Journal*, January, 1951.

This jolly Jack-O-Lantern is the only one known to the authors at this time. The overall shape is molded, however, not cut from an existing piece such as a bean pot. The face is cut after the Jack-O-Lantern was cast.

This cracker jar, the #100Z, is a real mystery. It features many embossed creatures resembling fossils, and a flag motif. It is marked on the bottom "100Z" and has been found listed in the 1962 production records. Surely the work of an outside designer unknown to us. 7" dia, 7 1/2" h w/lid.

The #92 Bird-Cage cookie jar. Listed in the 1958 catalog but not pictured, so we don't know if this is the correct lid. The #92 is identical to the #91 mold. This is the only one located by the authors.

EXPERIMENTAL DESIGNS

We refer to ware as being experimental if it appears to be an official product of the Watt Pottery. Trial patterns have several characteristics: (1) They are very professionally done, not casually. (2) The patterns, in keeping with production Watt patterns, are simple in nature and well suited to production. (3) Hopefully, they have been found on several shapes, not just a single piece. Other experimental wares are pieces known to be produced by the pottery as commemoratives, but not intended for production.

The first twelve pieces shown are a very important series. These 7 1/2" plates can be dated to around 1949 by the style of the leaves. These plates may be some of the original prototypes for the Watt hand-decorated patterns.

This trial pattern is similar to Rio Rose.

This trial pattern is essentially the Tropical pattern.

This trial pattern is basically original Starflower with an orange flower instead of a red one.

Another variation of Tropical.

A variation on a daisy-type flower. These leaves are more like the Daisy leaves than the previous two patterns.

The flowers in this pattern are similar to Daisy, but the leaves are much different.

A trial pattern with an unusual flower.

Another flower design like Daisy.

A blue version of the previous flower.

Red and white tulip trial pattern.

Red tulips with brown outlined leaves.

Trial pattern with multiple flowers.

SOUTH MOUNTAIN STONEWARE BY EVA ZEISEL

This 1955 experimental series is a very interesting combination of shapes developed by designer Eva Zeisel, and animal decorations designed by French artist, Michel Cadoret. The animals are called "Jungle Barnyard." The shapes became the Orchard Ware shapes in 1959, but the Jungle Barnyard decoration was not produced. The development of South Mountain Stoneware is covered in Chapter 2.

Left: Eva Zeisel #116 mug (3 1/4" dia, 5" h) in almond glaze with Jungle Barnyard decoration. This mug was not put into production. Right: #117 salt shaker in almond glaze. This is the original prototype piece for all Watt hourglass shakers.

Left: #110 covered baker. Right: #108 individual covered dish, both are clear glazed bowls with almond glazed lids and Jungle Barnyard decoration. These are the original prototypes for these bowl and lid designs. The #108 was not produced as a combination by the Watt Pottery. Its lid was used by Watt on the #01 grease jar, and the bowl became the #120 bowl.

Eva Zeisel #113 covered sugar in almond glaze and #114 creamer in clear glaze, both with Jungle Barnyard decoration. Neither piece saw production, although the lid is the prototype for the Watt #98 sugar bowl lid.

Eva Zeisel #102 luncheon plate in ivory glaze with Jungle Barnyard decoration.

Eva Zeisel designed, #112 teapot in almond glaze with Michel Cadoret's Jungle Barnyard decoration. Eva Zeisel's designs, marked "South Mountain Stoneware", are very important to the evolution of the shapes that the Watt Pottery produced. See Chapter 2 for a discussion of these pieces.

Clockwise, from top: #102 luncheon plate, almond glaze; #103 plate (6 1/4" dia), almond glaze; #104 saucer (6 1/4" dia), clear glaze; #103 plate, clear glaze. All pieces with Jungle Barnyard decoration.

Eva Zeisel #105 platter and #101 dinner plate, both in clear glaze with Jungle Barnyard decoration.

This swirl-glazed bean pot set is very beautifully done in blue, green, brown and cream glazes.

#75 bean cups in the "Confetti" pattern.

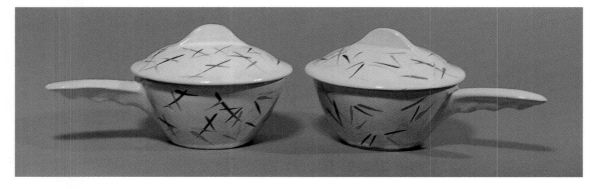

"Confetti" #18 casseroles.

This interesting 9" mixing bowl with bean pot handles was designed by Harry Watt. A small number were made, but it was not produced. Decorated with two-tone green leaves all around the bowl. Decorated by Ruth Russell.

A 9" batter bowl with pitcher handle. These were given to Watt foremen one year as a holiday gift. Decorated with a Starflower-type blossom in maroon glaze, and surrounded by brown leaves. The decoration continues all the way around the bowl.

A barrel bank. Decorated with a flower similar to the Cherry flower, with Starflower-type buds to the side.

#18 grooved handle casserole decorated with a strange-colored version of Rio Rose.

A very nice #15 pitcher with a band of crocuses and leaves around the middle.

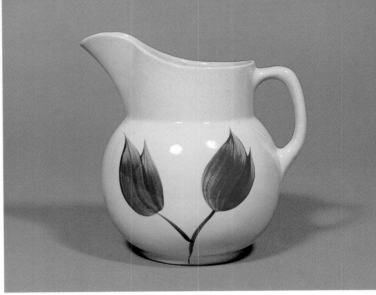

"Reduced Tulip" #16 pitcher. This could either be a mistake, or an attempt at a simpler Tulip pattern.

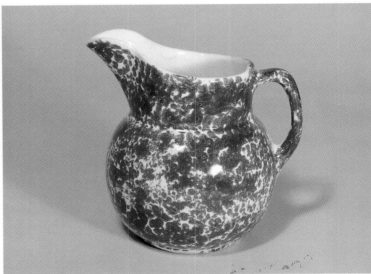

#16 pitcher with red sponge decoration over white glaze.

Ivy #62 creamer. A small number of other Ivy pieces have been found, including the sugar bowl and mugs.

#24 spaghetti bowl decorated with a Rio Rose flower on a Starflower stem. Signed, "Kate Russell May 5-54."

A #101 dinner plate with pastel rings.

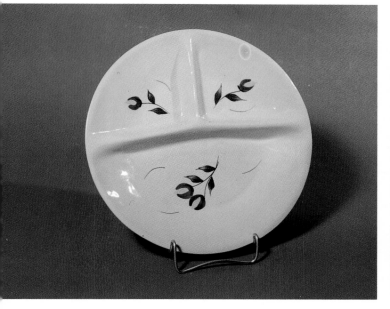

Divided dinner plate in a rosebud design.

#74 "Fiesta" bowl. These bowls are the only pieces found in this pattern so far.

#63 bowl, glaze sample kept by the Watt family.

ARTIST CUSTOMIZED WARE

These pieces are one of a kind pieces produced for personal use. They may vary in appearance from amateurish to very professional. In general, the finer pieces are far too complex to be considered for mass production. Some pieces may be signed under the glaze, or incised before firing. Artist customized Watt ware is highly prized by today's collectors.

A pair of #121 mugs with candle and holly decoration, designed to face left and right, and a #31 platter with candle and wreath decoration with a holly border.

#29 dinner plate with double flower design.

Rear view of the Christmas sugar and creamer set, showing the inscription, "Merry Christmas, 1957, The Watt Pottery Co."

Rear: a #49 chop plate with Christmas tree decoration and sponged border. The rim of the plate was turned-up extra deep at the request of the decorator, to allow baking in it. Front: 1957 Watt Christmas party creamer and sugars. The #75 bean cup was used as an open sugar bowl. These were favors at the 1957 Watt employee Christmas party, the only year this was done. Every other person at the tables got a creamer or sugar bowl. There were perhaps 50 sets produced. (The 1957 Christmas set is an official product, not just an artist-decorated set.)

1957 Christmas sugar bowl and a #121 Santa mug decorated for the Watt family.

#39 spaghetti bowl with a beautiful strawberry design. This may have been a test piece or a custom decoration.

#31 platter with holly and pine cone decoration. The decoration has a top and bottom to it.

#31 platter and #14 mixing bowl decorated for the 1957 employee Christmas party. Several of the decorators worked on this set.

#31 platter with fruit motif. Decorated by Ruth Russell.

#68 bowl with a cheerful pup!

#49 chop plate with a fish decoration. This plate features a deep rim to allow baking in it. The fish is a dark green.

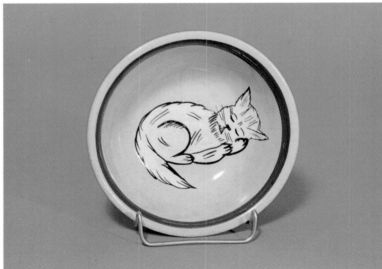

Sleeping kitty bowl, 5 1/2" dia, 2" h.

8 1/2" plate custom decorated for Bryce Watt.

Whimsical "Chef" salt and pepper shakers.

#49 Apple chop plate with green sponged edge.

#39 spaghetti bowl decorated with an apple with a worm greeting us with, "HI!."

#31 mugs with custom flower design. Reverse is marked, "Randy, 1962" on one and "Kevin, 1962" on the other. Decorated by Joy McGrath for her sons in Christmas, 1962.

#40 coffee cup with a handle different than the two production versions. The Gorsuch family supplied silica to the Watt Pottery for use in the glazes.

#96 bowl with berries in a wreath, and a red sponged edge.

#701 Apple mug with, "Marilyn" written above.

#121 "Pat" and "Marlin" mug.

This #69 refigerator pitcher is elaborately decorated on all sides.

#603 Mexican motif bowl with, "Randy."

Back side of the previous #69 pitcher.

Decorations under the spout of the same pitcher. There are red raspberries under the handle, also.

#15 pitcher with blue and green drip glaze.

Second set of bears. Curiously, the wording on the base was scraped off or filled-in before glazing. This set was in the office at the Watt Pottery for many years.

Pair of bears marked "Bear & Forebear, two little bears for every home." The reverse is marked, "Tom Watt, Aug 1929." From discussions with someone who talked to W.I. Watt about the bears, they represent Thomas and W.J. Watt. It is not known how many of these were made, this set was owned by Thomas Watt. The wording is in the mold. The bears are cast, and they are hollow with a closed base with a small central hole. 5 1/2" h, 3 5/8" w. base.

Reverse of second set of bears. The glaze is Watt brown.

Reverse of pair of bears in previous picture.

These 5" bowls were probably made for a restaurant. They have been found in several colors.

The #500 mug. Another mystery piece, as it doesn't seem to belong in with other Watt ware because of the barrel styling. Could there be a matching pitcher? 3 1/4" dia, 5" h, slightly taller tha a #501 mug.

Although made by another company for the Watt Pottery, one of these 3" paperweights would make a great addition to any collection.

The EZ-Mix bowl. Designed with two bases, one at an angle. When the bowl is placed on the second base, it is in a natural position for mixing. 8 1/2" dia, 5 1/2" h.

These towels and pot holders were used in an Ohio restaurant in the 1950s or 60s. Several sets are in collectors' hands today.

Throughout this book we have pictured metal accessory racks with
the ware they were intended to be used with. Here is an assortment of
stands and candle warmers to show the diversity of style which the
collector may encounter.

Chapter 30
Non Dinner Ware

Unlike many other potteries, Watt produced very little non-dinner ware. Several small lines of planters or jardinieres, some ash trays, animal dishes, and a pottery knife sharpener were the only non-dinner ware produced.

VASES, PLANTERS

Advertisement for 300 series planters with metal stands. Reprinted from the *Crockery and Glass Journal*, December, 1958.

300 series planters, quilted pattern, left to right: #302 (7" dia, 6 1/2" h), #301 (6" dia, 5" h).

#300 planter (4 1/2" dia, 4 1/2" h) on #904 wavy patterned base.

Bud vases. These are #126 cruets with the "V" and "O" removed from the mold. Left: bronze luster glaze. Right: experimental black glaze No. 9.

#902 green and #903 coral planters with flared bases.

Art Deco vase (4" dia, 6" h), spray brown glaze. NOTE: This vase was discussed with W.I. Watt and he confirmed that the pottery experimented with various vases similar to this one, but he did not personally inspect this vase. Not confirmed as Watt.

150 series planters, brown/white drip, left to right: #149 (4" dia, 3 1/2" h), #150 (5" dia, 4 1/2" h), #151 (6" dia, 5 1/2" h), #152 (7" dia, 6 1/2" h).

900 series planters, wavy pattern, left to right: #902 green with flared base (7 1/4" dia, 7" h), #901 white with straight base (6 1/4" dia, 7" h), #901 green with flared base (6 1/4" dia, 6" h), #903 yellow (6" dia, 5" h).

Mink feeding dishes, red, black and green raised letters, 9" dia. The
bottom is marked in the mold: "MAKERS OF MINK BREEDERS
CHOW AND MINK DEVELOPER CHOW MADE IN U.S.A." (see
Chapter 32 for bottom mark). There are rectangular Purina mink
dishes on the market with stencilled letters. We do not believe these
rectangular dishes are Watt.

#6 and #7 dog dishes in assorted colors.

#5 kitty bowls.

#504 spaniel dish,
6 1/2" dia.

Left to right: #6 dog dish (dog figures only), #62 kitten dish (5" dia, 1
1/2" h), #6 dog dish (dog figures and "DOG" lettering).

MISCELLANOUS

#95B ash tray, black glaze. These are official products, made from #95 bowls, the #94B was also made.

10 1/2" dia ash tray with Watt Pottery sample advertising. Also made in 4", 6" and 8" sizes.

#100 ash tray, bronze luster glaze. 8" dia, 2" h.

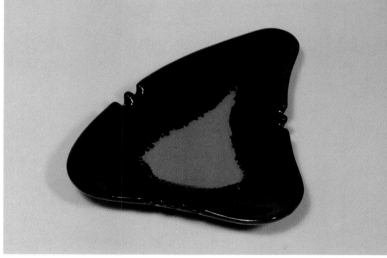

Ash tray made for the U.S. Ceramic Tile Company, teal and black glaze, 8" l, 6" w. Marked "Romany Spartan" in the mold.

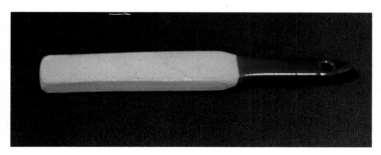

#90 knife sharpener, 8 1/2" l. Made with various solid color handles, and some striped handles.

The #90 knife sharpener was a premium, made available with advertising. Pictured is a salesman's sample.

Chapter 31
Guide to Trade Names

Trade names in this section are all found marked on the bottom of Watt ware. Watt ware was sold a number of different ways. Much of the pottery's output was distributed through supermarkets and chain stores. This ware was not necessarily marketed as Watt ware, but simply sold or given away as store premiums. Mr. Harold Hayes, a sales representative for the Watt Pottery, called this "supermarket-ware". This is one of the reasons why there are so many different marks on the bottoms of Watt ware. If a company ordered enough dinnerware, perhaps in a special pattern such as one of the many reduced decorations, a different version of the Watt mark helped track the ware from production through shipping. The trade names that we show listed by only the Watt Pottery were probably distributed as supermarket-ware.

In addition, the pottery often produced special series for other companies, and marked the bottom of the ware according to the specifications of the customer. Advertisements we have located for these lines list only the distributor's name and their name for the pattern or shape. The Watt Pottery advertised throughout the 1950s as a supplier of custom mold work. This flexibility gave them a great advantage over potteries that produced standard lines of ware and kept them in stock.

This listing covers only those trade names which are found marked in the mold.

AMERICAN HOMES This trade name was registered to Promotions Incorporated, of Youngstown, Ohio, in 1943. The company distributed ware using the names of leading magazines as trade names (*Cosmopolitan, Good Housekeeping*, etc). American Homes pieces are identical to Cabinart pieces, with 2-tone brown glaze.

BAK-EZEE One of the early kitchen and oven patterns. Found listed in the 1940 production records. Bake-Ezee is probably a Watt supermarket-ware brand name.

CABINART Listed by both Watt and the George Borgfeldt Corp. in 1944 and 1945. Most bottom marks are an intricate, embossed (raised) mark, featuring a cabin with smoke rising from the chimney. A few pieces have been found with an impressed mark. Found on a fairly extensive line of pieces including pitchers, creamers, cookie jars, pie plates and bean dishes, etc. Cabinart pieces are thick-walled, which are jigger-formed, not slip-cast. They are found primarily in 2-tone brown, but some are in single colors.

ESMOND Trade name of Esmond Industries, Inc. founded by Bennet Asquith. Esmond distributed ware from the 1950s through the 1980s. Esmond was produced by Watt, Purinton, McCoy and others.

EVE-N-BAKE A mark listed by Watt in 1946. The bottom mark for these pieces features a large, circular W with "Watt Ware" inscribed. Early pieces of Rio Rose and Red Apple may have this mark. There are two patterns *only* found on Eve-N-Bake pieces. We refer to them as the Eve-N-Bake patterns. All of these pieces have 4 embossed ridges running around the ware just above the bottom, and covered pieces have ridges on the lids. They are:

(1) Brown sprayed bands at the top and bottom of the pieces. NOTE: these are thin, sprayed bands, not brush-decorated.

(2) 3 white bands over yellow-ware color glaze (not the normal Watt cream color).

E-Z MIX A Watt trade name which is found only on a unique mixing bowl advertised in 1954. The bowls have small, embossed, vertical ribs and a flared rim. The unusual feature of these bowls is the two base areas underneath, one set at an angle to the other. When set on the second base, the bowl rests at an angle, making it easy to mix with.

FLAV-R-BAKE Another name listed only by Watt, from 1948 through 1958. It is the longest listed trade name that we can verify so far, although it is certainly not found as often as Eve-N-Bake.

GOLD-N-BAKE The last of the Bake-R Series. First listed by Watt in 1948. It is found marked primarily on blue/white banded ware.

HEIRLOOM STONEWARE Heirloom is a trade name of the Salem China Co, from Salem, Ohio. Watt produced this ware and it was sold as Salem. It has another interesting mark which features an impressed castle on larger pieces, and just "Heirloom" on the smaller molds. Mold numbers are in the 800 series. This is a complete line of embossed, basket-weave pottery, with plates, saucers, mugs, tumblers, casseroles, bean pots, and more. There are many shapes unique to Heirloom, but regular Watt molds such as pitchers and bean pots are modified with the basket-weave design.

J C STONEWARE This ware was distributed through a St. Louis supermarket chain, but we don't know which one yet. Found on basket-weave pieces in various colors, with mold numbers in the 800s, like Heirloom.

KATHY KALE Produced for the Kroger Co in 1965. Ware marked Kathy Kale was made by many potteries, but very little is Watt. Watt pieces feature an impressed chain pattern, fired with an off-white glaze.

KLA-HAM'RD A Watt trade name listed in 1944, which means: Clay...Hammered. A very short-lived pattern, produced for only a few months.

ORCHARD WARE Trade name used by ware distributed through Newland, Schneeloch and Piek, of New York City, from at least as early as the 1930s until recently. Their ware was produced by many china, pottery and glass companies. As marked on the pieces, Orchard Ware is a shape name, found on pieces ranging from mold #106 through #132. Orchard Ware molds are often found with a number of two-tone glazes where the top of the piece is dipped in a contrasting color glaze and allowed to flow down.

PEEDEECO Peedeeco stands for Pitman-Dreitzer and Co. of New York City. The company is currently a division of Lancaster Colony. Mr. Pitman and Mr. Dritzer have both passed away and no one in the company has been there long enough to remember the Watt connection. This is a nice line of pumpkin-shaped and colored pieces which includes bean pots and dishes, lug casseroles in several sizes, and a great pitcher.

R F SPAGHETTI This is Ravarino & Freschi Inc., located in St Louis. Found primarily on several sizes of spaghetti bowls and plates, usually in Rio Rose or Apple patterns.

SOUTH MOUNTAIN STONEWARE A line of ware designed by Eva Zeisel in late 1954, but never put into production. This is an ink-stamped bottom mark. The basic shapes of the ware became the Orchard Ware series in 1959.

Chapter 32
Guide to Bottom Marks

Most Watt ware is well marked. The greatest percentage of pieces even have the mold numbers marked, making identification easy. Watt, however, produced ware under at least 17 different trade names. The following photographs represent a selection of different marks. There are many more marks, but they are variations of the marks pictured, some with additional rings, fewer rings, etc. We believe the only significant marks we do not include are "Flav-R-Bake" and "EZ-Mix." Watt ware can also be found with foil stickers on the bottom. These stickers feature the eagle corporate emblem.

Early kitchen and oven ware mark variation, c. 1940.

Early kitchen and oven ware mark, full mark, c. 1940.

Early kitchen and oven ware mark, size only, c. 1940.

Moon & Stars pieces are found unmarked, c. 1940

Bak-Ezee mark, early banded ware c. 1940.

Cabinart embossed mark, c. 1944.

Kla-Ham'rd mark, c. 1944.

Unusual impressed Cabinart mark, c. 1944.

Peedeeco mark, stands for Pitman-Dreitzer and Company, c. 1940s.

American Homes mark, pieces are the same as Cabinart ware, c. 1940s.

Eve-N-Bake mark, late 1940s.

Gold-N-Bake mark, late 1940s.

Large "W" and "Watt Ware" mark, late 1940s.

Large "W" mark, late 1940s.

Script "Oven Ware" and script "Watt", early 1950s.

Script "Oven Ware".

"R-F Spaghetti" mark. Trade name for Ravarino and Freschi Inc.

Script "Watt", early 1950s.

Block "Oven Ware".

Block "Watt".

Block "Watt" and block "Oven Ware".

Mold number and "U.S.A." only.

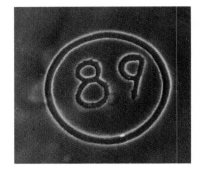

Mold number only.

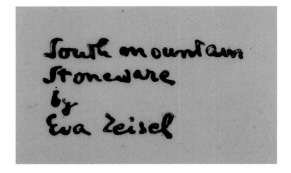

"South Mountain Stoneware" ink mark. Eva Zeisel designed ware, c. 1954. Very rare mark.

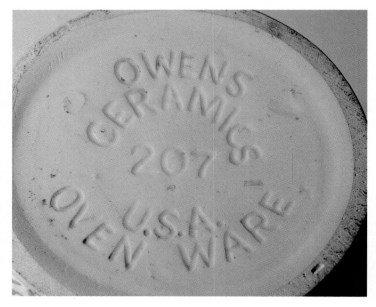

"Owens" 200 series mark found on Wood Grain pieces produced for Owens Ceramics, c. 1958.

200 series mark with "Watt", found on pieces in Owens Wood Grain, c. 1958.

"Orchard Ware" mark, found on mold numbers from #106 to #132, 1960s.

"ESMOND" mark found on ware produced for Esmond Industries, c. 1960. Note: see chapter 19 for marks which are not-Watt.

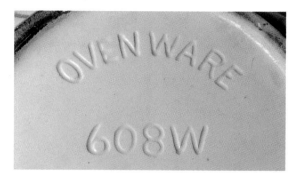

600 series mark found on Wood Grain, 1960s.

800 series "J.C. Stoneware" mark found on Basket Weave pieces produced for another company.

"Heirloom Stoneware", full mark. Found on basket weave ware produced for Salem China Co.

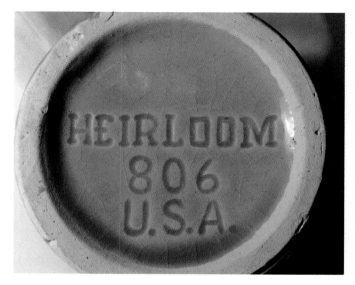

"Heirloom" only mark, found on smaller pieces produced for Salem China Co.

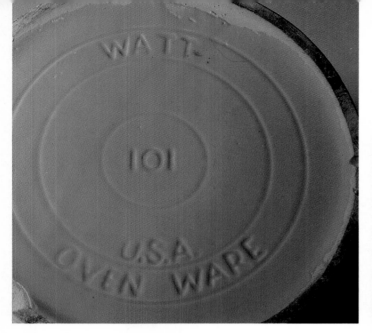

100 series mark found on Basket Weave pieces.

Ice tea keg mark.

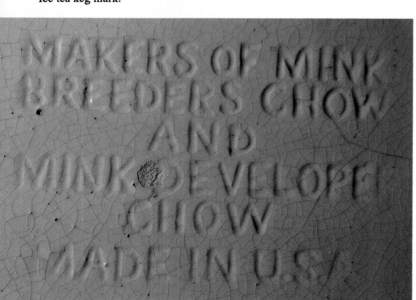

Mark found on mink dishes.

Mark found on Romany Spartan ash tray made for U.S. Ceramic Tile Co.

"Kathy Kale" mark found on Royal Danish ware, c. 1965. Other potteries' marks are identical, see chapter 25.

Chapter 33
Guide to Mold Numbers

This section of the book is designed to help collectors identify the many molds which were used by the Watt Pottery. The first list is a master reference which contains all mold numbers known to the authors, listed in numerical order. This will refer the reader to: (1) One of the specific lists in this chapter containing complete descriptions of the sizes and uses of the pieces. (2) A chapter which describes the piece in more detail if it is a non-standard mold number (such as a Basket Weave piece).

The specific lists are grouped by pieces with shapes in common, such as pitchers, mixing bowls, etc. These lists mainly cover the Watt ware decorated in the classic and modern patterns. Non-standard mold numbers are described in separate chapters.

To find a particular piece by shape (pitcher, mixing bowl, etc.), look in the list which contains those types of pieces. To identify a piece knowing only the mold number, look up the number in the first list and refer to the section indicated.

Note: Listed diameters are the top diameters of the piece, without handles or spouts.

MOLD #   SPECIFIC LIST OR CHAPTER

MOLD #	SPECIFIC LIST OR CHAPTER
01	Cookie Jars, Bean Pots, Canisters
02	Cookie Jars, Bean Pots, Canisters
04 to 07	Bowls, Bakers
1	Bowls, Bakers
4	Bowls, Bakers
6	Bowls, Bakers
7	Bowls, Bakers
8	Bowls, Bakers (Also see Covered Casseroles)
5- 14	Mixing Bowls
15 - 17	Pitchers, Tea Pots, Carafes
16	See Chapter 19 on Esmond ware
18	Bowls, Bakers (Also see Covered Casseroles)
3/19	Covered Casseroles
20	Covered Casseroles
21	Cookie Jars, Bean Pots, Canisters
22-25	Bowls, Bakers
27 - 31	Plates, Saucers
30, 32	See Chapter 19 on Esmond ware
31	Cups, Mugs, Sugar and Creamers
33	Miscellaneous Dinner Ware
34	See Chapter 19 on Esmond ware
35	Cups, Mugs, Sugar and Creamers
36, 37	See Chapter 19 on Esmond ware
39	Bowls, Bakers
40	Cups, Mugs, Sugar and Creamers
41 - 43	Plates, Saucers
43-1-43-19	See Kla-Ham'rd section in Chapter 5
44	Bowls, Bakers
45, 46	Miscellaneous dinner ware
47	Cookie Jars, Bean Pots, Canisters
48	Cups, Mugs, Sugar and Creamers
2/48	Covered Casseroles
49	Plates, Saucers
50 - 55	Bowls, Bakers (Also see Covered Casseroles)
56	Cups, Mugs, Sugar and Creamers
58	Bowls, Bakers
59	Cookie Jars, Bean Pots, Canisters
60	Bowls, Bakers
61	Cups, Mugs, Sugar and Creamers (Also see Mixing Bowls)

MOLD #	SPECIFIC LIST OR CHAPTER
62	Cups, Mugs, Sugar and Creamers (Also see animal dishes in Chapter 30 and Esmond ware in Chapter 19)
63 - 65	Mixing Bowls
66 - 68	Bowls, Bakers (Also see Covered Casseroles)
69	Pitchers
70	Covered Casseroles
71	Miscellaneous Non-Dinner Ware
72	Cookie Jars, Bean Pots, Canisters
73 - 75	Bowls, Bakers (Also see Covered Casseroles)
76	Cookie Jars, Bean Pots, Canisters
77	Bowls, Bakers
80 - 82	Cookie Jars, Bean Pots, Canisters
84	Covered Casseroles
85	Bowls, Bakers
86	Covered Casseroles
87 - 89	Bowls, Bakers
90	Miscellaneous Dinner Ware
91 - 93	Cookie Jars, Bean Pots, Canisters
94 - 96	Bowls, Bakers (Also see Covered Casseroles)
94 - 98	See Chapter 14 on Morning Glory
94, 95	See ash trays in Chapter 30
98	Cups, Mugs, Sugar and Creamers
99	See Chapter 23 on Basket Weave
100	See ash trays in Chapter 30
100Z	Cookie Jars, Bean Pots, Canisters
100 - 102	See Chapter 23 on Basket Weave
101 - 105	Plates, Saucers
106	Bowls, Bakers
110	Covered Casseroles
112	Pitchers, Tea Pots, Carafes
115	Pitchers, Tea Pots, Carafes
117, 118	Miscellaneous Dinner Ware
119, 120	Bowls, Bakers
121	Cups, Mugs, Sugar and Creamers
123 - 125	See Chapter 23 on Basket Weave
126	Miscellaneous Dinner Ware
127	See Chapter 23 on Basket Weave
130, 131	Covered Casseroles
132	Pitchers, Tea Pots, Carafes
133	Miscellaneous Dinner Ware
149 - 152	See planters in Chapter 30
200 - 208	See Chapter 24 on Owen's Wood Grain ware
300 - 305	See planters in Chapter 30
400, 401	See ice tea kegs in Chapter 24
500, 501	Cups, Mugs, Sugar and Creamers
502, 503	Cookie Jars, Bean Pots, Canisters
504	See animal dishes in Chapter 30
505	Pitchers, Tea Pots, Carafes
506	Covered Casseroles
600 - 604	Bowls, Bakers (Also see Covered Casseroles)
616	Mixing Bowls
605W-627W	See Chapter 24 on Wood Grain
801 - 816	See Chapter 23 on Basket Weave
900 - 904	See planters in Chapter 30

BOWLS, BAKERS

04	Nappy, rounded, top ribs, 4 1/4" d, 2" h
05	Nappy, rounded, top ribs, 5 1/4" d, 2 1/2" h (also covered)
06	Nappy, rounded, top ribs, 6 1/4" d, 3" h
07	Nappy, rounded, top ribs, 7 1/4" d, 3 3/4" h
1	Bowl, lip & shoulder, 5 3/4" d, 2 1/4" h
4	Bowl, 5" d, 1 3/4" h ("Nuts" bowl)
6	Bowl, 6 1/4" d, 2 1/4" h (same as 52)

7	Bowl, 7" d, 2 3/4" h ("Chips" bowl)
8	Bowl, lip & shoulder, 8 3/4" d, 3 1/4" h
18	12 ounce handled bowl, 5" d, 2 1/4"h (lug or tab handles - also covered)
22	Berry bowl, lipped, 5 1/2" d, 2" h
23	Individual salad bowl, 5 5/8" d, 1 1/2" h
24	Spaghetti bowl, lip, 11" d, 2 1/2" h
25	Spaghetti bowl, lip, 15" d, 3 1/2" h
39	Spaghetti bowl, lip, 13" d, 3 1/4" h
39	Spaghetti bowl, straight sides, 13" d, 3 1/4" h
44	Flat soup bowl, lip, 8" d, 1 1/2" h
50	Spaghetti bowl, lip, 10 1/4" d, 2 1/4" h
52	Individual salad bowl, 6 1/4" d, 2 1/4" h ("Corn" bowl)
53	Baker, 7 1/4" d, 3" h (Also covered)
54	Baker, 8 1/4" d, 3 1/4" h ("Pretzels" bowl, also covered)
55	Salad bowl, 11 3/4" d, 4" h
58	Fruit or salad bowl, tall base, 10 1/2" d, 3 3/4" h
60	Baker, 6 1/4"d, 2 3/8" h
66	Baker, 7 1/4" d, 3 1/2" h (Also covered)
67	Baker, 8 1/4" d, 3 1/2" h (Also covered)
68	Baker, 5 1/4" d, 4" h
73	Salad bowl, 9 1/2" d, 4" h (Also covered)
74	Individual salad bowl, 5 1/2" d, 2" h
75	8 ounce bean cup, 3 1/2" d, 2 1/4" h (Also covered)
77	16 ounce bean cup, 4 1/4" d, 3" h (Also covered)
85	Rectangular baker, tab handles, 9" l, 5 1/2" w, 2 1/2" h
87	(Alternate number for #18, but probably not marked "87")
88	Pointed oval "canoe" bowl, 6 1/2" l, 5" w, 2 1/2" h
89	Pointed oval "canoe" bowl, 11" l, 8 3/4" w, 3 3/4" h
94	Baker or indiv. salad bowl, 6" d, 1 3/4" h
95	Baker, 7 1/4" d, 2 1/4" h
96	Baker, 8 1/2" d, 2 3/4" h (Also covered)
106	Salad bowl, tall base, 10 3/4" d, 3 3/4" h
119	Salad or chip bowl, 9" d, 3 1/2" h
120	Indiv. salad bowl (plain base), 5" d, 2" h
120	Dip bowl, (recessed base), 5" d, 2" h
600	Ribbed nappy, straight side, 7 3/4" d, 3" h (Also covered)
601	Ribbed nappy, straight side, 8 3/4" d, 3 1/2" h (Also covered)
602	Ribbed nappy, straight side, 4 3/4" d, 1 1/2" h
603	Ribbed nappy, straight side, 5 3/4" d, 2" h
604	Ribbed nappy, straight side, 6 3/4" d, 2 1/2" h

COVERED CASSEROLES

05	Ribbed nappy, dome lid, 5" d, 2 1/2" h, 4" h with lid
8	Old casserole, 4 tab handles or no handles, recessed flattened dome lid, 8 3/4" d, 3 1/4" h, 4 1/2" h with lid
18	Individual casserole, 2 tab handles, sold with dome lid/button knob or #01 funnel lid, 5" d, 2 1/4" h, 3 3/4" h with lid (sometimes marked "18N")
18	Individual casserole, grooved handle, dome lid/button knob, 5" d, 2 1/4" h, 3 3/4" h with lid
18	Individual casserole, French handle, sold with dome lid with blade or button knob, 5" d, 2 1/4" h, 4" h with lid
18	Old style individual casserole, oval handle, dome lid with button knob, 5" d, 2" h, 3 3/4" h with lid
3/19	Casserole, flattened dome lid with rim (bowl may be recessed for lid or not), 9" d, 3" h, 5 1/4" h with lid
20	Roaster, recessed flattened dome lid, 10 1/2" d, 4" h, 7" h with lid
2/48	Casserole, recessed flattened dome lid, 7 1/2" d, 2 3/4" h, 3 3/4" h with lid
53	Covered baker, flattened dome lid, 7 1/2" d, 3" h, 5 1/4" h / lid
54	Covered baker, flattened dome lid, 8 1/2" d, 3 1/2" h, 6" h / lid
66	Covered baker, dome lid, 7 1/4" d, 3" h, 5 1/2" h with lid

67	Covered baker, dome lid, 8 1/4" d, 3 1/2" h, 6 1/2" h with lid
70	Dutch oven, dome lid, 9 1/2" d, 4 1/2" h, 7 1/4" h with lid
73	Covered salad bowl, "upside-down pie plate" lid, 9 1/2" d, 4" h, 6" h with lid
84	Square baker, 8" square, 6" h with lid
86	Oval baker, tab handles, blade handle on lid, 10" l, 5" h with lid
96	Covered baker, funnel lid (large or small knob), 8 1/2" d, 2 3/4" h, 5 3/4" h with lid (Note - lid fits #110, #130, #131 also)
110	Covered baker, funnel lid (large or small knob), 8 1/2" d, 3 3/4" h, 6 3/4" h with lid (Note - lid fits #96, #130, #131 also)
130	Tureen, funnel lid (large or small knob, lid may have cut-out for ladle), 8 1/2" d, 5" h, 8" h with lid (Note - lid fits #96, #110, #131 also)
131	Covered bowl, funnel lid (large or small knob), 8 1/2" d, 3 3/4" h, 6" h with lid (Note - lid fits #96, #110, #130 also)
506	Lug handle casserole (fondue), dome lid, 6" d, 2 1/2" h, 4 1/4" h with lid
600	Ribbed covered baker, ribbed lid, 7 3/4" d, 3" h, 5 1/4" h with lid
601	Ribbed covered baker, ribbed lid, 8 3/4" d, 3 1/2" h, 6 1/4" h with lid

MIXING BOWLS

5	5" Mixing bowl (lip, lip & shoulder, or ribbed)
6	6" Mixing bowl (lip, lip & shoulder, or ribbed)
7	7" Mixing bowl (lip, lip & shoulder, or ribbed)
8	8" Mixing bowl (lip, lip & shoulder, or ribbed)
9	9" Mixing bowl (lip, lip & shoulder, or ribbed)
10	10" Mixing bowl, lip & shoulder
11	11" Mixing bowl, lip & shoulder
12	12" Mixing bowl, lip & shoulder
14	14" Mixing bowl, lip & shoulder
616	16" Mixing bowl, lip & shoulder
61	1 pint deep mixing bowl, 5 1/2" d, 3 3/4" h
63	2 pint deep mixing bowl, 6 1/2"d, 4 1/4" h
64	4 pint deep mixing bowl, 7 1/2" d, 4 3/4" h
65	6 pint deep mixing bowl, 9" d, 5" h
?	Old style deep mixing bowl, lip and shoulder, 6" d, 4" h
?	Old style deep mixing bowl, lip and shoulder, 8" d, 5 1/2" h
?	Old style deep mixing bowl, lip and shoulder, 10" d, 6 1/2" h

COOKIE JARS, BEAN POTS, CANISTERS

01	Grease jar, funnel lid, 5" d, 3 1/2" h, 5" h with lid
02	2 section stacking refrigerator set, flat lid, 7 1/2" d, 7" h with lid
21	Barrel cookie jar, flattened dome lid, 7" d, 6" h, 7 1/2" h with lid
47	Grease jar, dome lid with ridge, 4 1/2" d, 4" h, 5" h with lid
59	Ice bucket, flat lid, 7 1/2" d, 5 3/4" h, 7" h with lid
59	"Goodies" jar, domed lid, same as ice bucket except 8 1/2" h with lid
72	Large cookie canister, dome lid, 7 1/4" d, 6 3/4" h, 9" h with lid (same lid as #66 covered baker)
72	Curved side, tapered "Goodies" jar, dome lid, 7 1/4" d, 7 1/4" h, 9 1/2" h with lid (same lid as #66 covered baker)
76	2 1/2 quart bean pot, ear handles, 5 1/2" d, 6 1/2" h with lid
80	Cheese crock, flattened dome lid with rim, 8 1/2" d, 8" h
81	Canister, dome lid, 6 1/2" d ("Flour" & "Sugar" canister)
82	Canister, dome lid, 5" d, ("Coffee" & "Tea" canister)
91	Tapered cookie jar, cone top, 7 1/2" d, 7" h, 10 3/4" h with lid
92	Tapered cookie jar, same as #91
93	1 1/2" quart bean pot, ear handles, 5" d, 5 1/2" h with lid
100Z	Cookie jar with embosssed creatures, 7 " d, 7 1/2" h with lid
502	4 quart bean pot, ear handles, 6 1/2" d, 7 1/2" h with lid
503	Cookie jar, ear handles, 6 1/2" d, 8" h with lid

PITCHERS, TEA POTS, CARAFES

?	Old style pitcher, 4 pint, 7" h
15	1 pint pitcher, 5 1/4" h
16	2 pint pitcher, 6 1/2" h
17	5 pint pitcher, ice lip or plain lip, 8" h
62	1/2 pint creamer, 4 1/4" h
69	Square refigerator pitcher, ice lip, 8" h
112	Tea pot, 6-cup, disc lid (same lid as #98), 6" h with lid
115	Coffee server, 60-ounce, small handle, lid with flat blade handle, 10 1/2" h with lid
115	Carafe, 60-ounce, long ribbon handle, no lid, 9 1/2" h
115	Carafe, 60-ounce, no handle, no spout, no lid, 9 1/4" h
132	Carafe, lid with round knob, 10 1/2" h
505	Tea pot, 32-ounce, lid with flat blade handle, 5 3/4" h

CUPS, MUGS, SUGAR and CREAMERS

31	Esmond mug, curved waist, 3 1/2" d, 3 1/2" h
?	Sugar bowl to match #40 cup
35	Creamer to match #40 cup
40	Coffee cup, small, (handle may be round ring, "D" ring, or flat blade with hole), 3" d, 2 3/4" h, 2" d base
?	Coffee cup, large, ring handle, 4" d, 2 3/4" h, 2" d base
?	Sugar bowl to match large coffee cup
?	Creamer to match large coffee cup
48	Stacking creamer (small), flat lid with groove, 3 3/4" d, 2 3/4" h
48	Stacking creamer (medium), flat lid with groove, 4" d, 3 1/4" h
48	Stacking creamer (large), flat lid with groove, 4 1/2" d, 3 3/4" h
56	Tumbler, rounded sides, 3 1/2" d, 4" h
56	Tumbler, straight sides, 4" d, 4 1/2" h
61	Coffee mug, short, 3 1/4" d, 3" h
62	1/2 pint creamer, 4 1/4" h
98	Sugar bowl, disc lid (same lid as #112), 3 1/2" d, 4 1/4" h, 4 1/2" h with lid

121	Coffee mug, hourglass, 3" d, 3 3/4" h
500	Barrel mug, 3 1/4" d, 5" h
501	Beer mug, bulged waist, 2 3/4" d, 4 1/2" h
701	Coffee mug, slant sides, blade handle, 3 1/2" d, 3 3/4" h

PLATES, SAUCERS

27	Deep saucer for large cup, 6 1/2" d, 1 1/4" h, 2 3/4" base, 2 1/4" cup ring
27	Flat saucer for large cup, 6 1/2" d, 1" h, 3 1/4" base, 2 1/4" cup ring
28	Salad plate, 7 1/2"d
29	Dinner plate, 9 1/2" d
30	Snack plate with offset cup ring, 11 1/2"d
31	Chop/pizza plate, 15" d, (Also called #105)
41	Saucer for #40 cup, 5 3/4" d, 2 3/4" base, 2 1/8" cup ring
42	Salad plate, 6 1/2" d,
43	Luncheon plate, 8 3/4" d
49	Sandwich/chop plate, 12" d
101	Dinner plate, 10" d
102	Luncheon plate, 7 1/2" d
103	Salad plate, 6 1/2" d
105	Chop/pizza platter, 15" d

MISCELLANEOUS DINNER WARE

33	Pie plate, 9 1/4" d
45	Barrel salt shaker, 2 1/2" d, 4" h
46	Barrel pepper shaker, 2 1/2" d, 4" h
90	Knife sharpener, 8 1/2" l, 1 1/4" w
117	Salt shaker, hourglass (raised "S" or holes in "S" pattern), 2 1/4" d, 4 3/4" h
118	Pepper shaker, hourglass (raised "P" or holes in "P" pattern), 2 1/4" d, 4 3/4" h
126	Vinegar and oil cruets with lids, hourglass, 2" d, 7 1/2" h with lid
133	Electric warmer base (solid or cut-away base)

BIBLIOGRAPHY

Crockery and Glass Journal, The. East Stroudsburg, PA: Haire Publishing Co., 1940-1961.

Crooks, Guy E. *History of Crooksville Ohio.* Crooksville, OH: Crooksville Lions Club, 1945.

Lehner, Lois. *Lehner's Encyclopedia of U.S. Marks On Pottery, Porcelain & Clay.* Paducah, KY: Schroeder Publishing Co., 1988.

Lehner, Lois. *Ohio Pottery and Glass, Marks and Manufacturers.* Des Moines, IA: Wallace-Homestead Book Co., 1978.

Le Château Dufrense, Inc., Musée des Arts Décoratifs de Montréal. *Eva Zeisel: Designer For Industry.* Chicago, IL: 1984.

Morris, Sue and Dave. *Watt Pottery, An Identification and Value Guide.* Paducah, KY: Schroeder Publishing Co., 1992.

Sanford, Martha and Steve. *The Guide to Brush-McCoy Pottery.* Martha and Steve Sanford, 1992.

Staff. "New Tableware Made From Native Perry County Clay," *Sunday Times-Signal, The.* (June 26, 1949): Sec. 4, p. 7.

Tyacke, Marvin and Beverly. "Watt Pottery," *The Antique Trader Weekly* (September 13, 1978): 66-67.

Watt, William Iliff. *Collectibles* 2. Zanesville, OH: 1988.

Watt, William Iliff. "Pottery maker describes famous patterns used," *Perry County Tribune* (July 16, 1986): 11.

OTHER REFERENCES

Columbus Evening Dispatch, The. (June 17, 1950).

Hayes, Harold. Private correspondence and conversations.

Ogden, Jim and Carol. Private conversations.

Thompson, Dennis M. *Spoutings* (Box 26067, Fairview Park, OH 44126) A quarterly newsletter, nos. 1-6, 1992-1993.

Watt Pottery Company, The. Corporate records (Official Records of Proceedings, minutes, payroll records), photos, legal papers, catalogs, price sheets, production records.

Zanesville News, The. (June 17, 1950).

Zanesville Signal, The. (June 17-18, 1950).

> ### Collectors' Associations
>
> **Watt Pottery Collectors USA:** Box 26067; Fairview Park OH 44126
> The quarterly newsletter, *Spoutings,* is written by author Dennis M. Thompson. A one-year subscription is $12.00.
>
> **Watt Collectors Association:** Box 184; Galesburg IL 61402-0184
> Yearly dues are $10.00, which includes the quarterly newsletter, *Watt's News.*

Price Guide

In an attempt to reflect actual current prices of Watt ware prices have been gathered from collectors, antique shows and shops, dealer surveys and auctions across the country. Many of the rarer items have primarily sold at auctions where prices vary widely. We have marked these prices with **.

Listed prices are retail selling prices for pieces in excellent condition from dealers or auctions. Sales between individuals do not necessarily bring full retail prices. Factory flaws, such as glaze imperfections, off-center patterns, etc. are minor flaws in Watt ware, although the value of such pieces may be reduced. Minor flaws from usage, should certainly lower value somewhat. Oil spots and stains call for greater reduction. More serious damage such as cracks and chips should receive significant reductions in value for all but the rarest pieces. Items photographed with metal stands, candle warmers, etc. are priced without the stands, unless stated. Metal stands are priced from $35.00 to $100.00 each, depending on the exact style. (See page 223). A simple metal stand is a minimum price, while a stand with a candle warmer would bring much more. Advertising stamped on the pottery may increase the value of Watt ware, however many collectors prefer pieces without advertising. The following is an approximate guide to the value of advertising ware:

Shakers, pitchers, and common bowls: Add up to 10%.
Cookie jars, casseroles (outside adv.), etc: Add 10% to 15%.
Salesman samples: Add 25% (for bowls) to 50%.
Apple dinner plates: Apple plates with advertising are much more common and less valuable than plain plates.

The following notations are used in this price guide:

**	Prices were obtained from auctions or unique transactions.	est.	Authors' estimated price based on similar pieces.
ea.	Prices are for one piece, not a set.	NA	Not Available - limited production item has not sold recently.

PAGE	DESCRIPTION	VALUE	PAGE	DESCRIPTION	VALUE	PAGE	DESCRIPTION	VALUE
37-39	Crocks, jugs	$50-$150	59	#15 Rio Rose pitcher	$125-$200	70	#8 Daisy casserole	$75-$100
39	Churns, coolers	$100-$200	59	#16 Rio Rose pitcher	$100-$125	70	Old style #18 Daisy casserole	$100-$135
40	Loops mixing bowls	$15-$25	59	#17 Rio Rose pitcher	$165-$200	70	#40 Daisy cup and #41 saucer	$85-$100
41	Loops casseroles	$40-$50	59	#21 Raised Rose & Rio Rose cookie jars	$135-$175 ea.	70	#24 Daisy spaghetti bowl	$60-$80
41	Loops lug casseroles	$15-$25	59	#72 Rio Rose canister	$300-$400	70	#23 Daisy bowls	$25-$40
41	Arcs casseroles	$40-$50	59	#18 Rio Rose casserole	$100-$125	71	#69 5-petal casserole	$500 est.
41	Custard cups	$25-$35	59	Old style Rio Rose casserole	$75-$100	71	#72 4-petal canister	$350 est.
42	Arcs casseroles	$40-$50	59	8" & #2/48 Rio Rose casserole	$50-$70	72	#69 4-petal refrigerator pitcher	$775 **
42	Arcs mixing bowls	$15-$25	59	#20 Rio Rose roaster	$75-$125	72	#62 4-petal creamer	$200-$275
42	Pie plates	$35-$50	60	Rio Rose mixing bowls	$25-$50	72	#15 4-petal pitcher	$150-$190
42	Raised Button lug casseroles	$20-$30	60	Large cup and #27 saucer	$85-$100	72	#16 4-petal pitcher	$80-$90
43	Moon & Stars casseroles	$50-$75	60	#40 cup and #41 saucer	$85-$100	72	#17 4-petal ice-lip pitcher	$160-$190
43	Moon & Stars bowls	$25-$60	60	Sugar bowl	$100-$125	72	#62 5-petal creamer	$150-$175
43	Arcs canister	$85-$100	60	#27 saucers	$15-$25	72	#15 5-petal pitcher	$65-$85
43	Moon & Stars canister	$100-$125	60	Indiv. Rio Rose bowls	$20-$35	72	#16 5-petal pitcher	$80-$90
44	Moon & Stars pitcher	$50-$75	60	#31 Rio Rose platter	$75-$90	72	#17 5-petal plain-lip pitcher	$160-$190
44	Creamer, Moon & Stars variation	$100 est.	60	#49 Rio Rose plate	$50-$60	72	#56 5-petal tumbler	$325-$425 **
44	Moon & Stars small pitcher	$100 est.	60	#28 & #42 Rio Rose plates	$30-$45	72	#501 4-petal mug	$80-$90
44	5" Moon & Stars bowl	$25-$30	61	#39 & #25 Rio Rose spaghetti bowls	$70-$90	72	#61 5-petal mug	$135-$175
44	Bean pot set	$75-$100	61	#24 Rio Rose spaghetti bowl	$60-$80	72	#62 4-petal creamer	$200-$275
45	Diamond casseroles	$50-$75	61	#23 salad bowl	$20-$35	72	#62 5-petal creamer	$150-$175
45	Bak-Ezee casserole	$35-$60	61	#44 flat soup bowl	$20-$35	72	#98 sugar bowl, open	$150-$200
45	Bak-Ezee bowls	$15-$30	61	#22 Bullseye berry bowl	$20-$35	72	#98 sugar bowl, covered	$350 est.
45	Bak-Ezee pie plate	$20-$35	61	#31 Bullseye platter	$75-$100	73	#115 4-petal coffee carafe	$1500 **
46	Lug casseroles	$25-$40	61	#28 Bullseye plate	$30-$45	73	#117 and #118 4-petal shakers	$150-$200
46	Embossed Wreath nappies	$20-$40	61	Bullseye cup and saucer	$85-$100	73	#01 4-petal grease jar	$300-$350
47	Blue Embossed Wreath nappy	$50-$85	62	#30 Snack plate & #24 spaghetti bowl	$60-$80	73	#45 and #46 5-petal shakers	$85-$100
47	#43-19 pitcher	$65-$85	62	#28 plate	$30-$45	73	#47 5-petal grease jar	$325-$425 **
47	S-M-L refrigerator set	$25-$40 ea.	62	#25 spaghetti bowl	$70-$90	73	#80 4-petal cheese crock	$275-$350
48	#43-13 pie plate	$40-$50	62	#33 pie plate	$110-$135	73	#96 4-petal covered baker	$100-$125
48	#43-15, 16, 17 mixing bowls	$20-$25	62	#44 flat soup bowls	$20-$35	73	#8182 4-petal canister set	$350-$425 ea.
48	#43-18 bean pot	$50-$60	62	#25 spaghetti bowl	$70-$90	74	#67 covered bakers	$100-$125
48	#43-12 casserole	$35-$50	63	#4 Tropical bowl	$200 est.	74	#503 4-petal cookie jar	$400 est.
48	#43-11, 43-4-6, & 43-8-10 casserole	$25-$35 ea.	63	10" Tropical plate	$400 est.	74	#76 4-petal bean pot	$110-$140
48	#43-2	$15-$20	63	#45, #46 Original Starflower shakers	$750 **	74	#75 4-petal bean cups	$35-$45
48	Small hammered bowl	$85 est	64	#31 Original Starflower platter	$300 est.	74	#18 4-petal tab handle casserole	$110-$130
49	Cabinart creamers	$30-$40	64	#39 Moonflower spaghetti bowl	$100-$125	74	#31 5-petal platter	$135-$175
49	Cabinart sugar bowl	$80-$100	64	#22 Moonflower berry bowl	$20-$30	74	#49 5-petal plate	$125-$150
49	Cabinart tall ice-lip pitcher	$75-$90	64	#31 Moonflower platter	$85-$110	74	#33 4-petal pie plate	$150-$175
49	Cabinart small pitcher	$25-$30	64	#101 Moonflower plate	$50-$75	75	#25 5-petal spaghetti bowl	$75-$100
49-50	Cabinart jars & bakers	$25-$65	64	Moonflower cup & saucer	$85-$100	75	#18 5-petal groove handle casserole	$110-$130
50	Cabinart pie plate	$35-$50	65	#18 Moonflower casseroles	$100-$135	75	#21 5-petal cookie jar	$200-$250
50	Cabinart custard cups	$15-$30	65	Old style #18 casseroles	$100-$135	75	#76 4-petal bean pot	$110-$140
50	Mixing bowls	$15-$25	65	Moonflower creamer and sugar	$125-$150 ea.	75	#59 ice buckets	$150-$200
51	Swirl mixing bowls	$25-$45	65	#101 Moonflower plate	$50-$75	75	8" 5-petal baker	$30-$40
51	Swirl pie plates	$40-$65	65	#21 Moonflower cookie jars	$150-$200	75	#18 5-petal tab handle casserole	$110-$130
51	#7 Swirl casserole	$50-$75	65	8" Moonflower casserole	$35-$50	75	#52 - #54 5-petal bowls	$35-$45
52	Peedeeco pitcher	$85-$125	66	Wooden carousel and bowls	$200-$400	75	#63 - #65 deep mixing bowls	$40-$60
52	Peedeeco bean pot	$50-$60	66	Moonflower cups and saucers	$85-$100	76	Boxed salad set	$300-$775 **
52	Peedeeco bean cups	$5-$10	66	Moonflower creamer and sugar	$125-$150 ea.	76	#50 5-petal spaghetti bowl	$175-$200
52	Peedeeco 5" casserole	$35-$50	66	#42 Moonflower plate	$35-$50	76	#60 5-petal (inside)	$75-$90
52	Peedeeco 8" casserole	$50-$75	66	#101 Moonflower plate	$50-$75	76	#55 salad bowl	$85-$120
53	Eve-N-Bake casseroles, bakers	$20-$45	67	#31 Moonflower platter	$85-$110	76	#73 salad bowl	$90-$120
53	Eve-N-Bake pitcher	$75-$100	67	#18 Moonflower casserole	$100-$135	76	#4 salad bowl	$30-$40
53	Eve-N-Bake mixing bowls	$20-$30	67	#101 Moonflower plate	$50-$75	77	#60 - #68 5-petal bowls	$30-$60
54	#21 Eve-N-Bake cookie jar	$50-$75	67	#24 Moonflower spaghetti bowl	$85-$100	77	#04 - #07 4-petal nappies	$35-$50
54	Eve-N-Bake pitcher	$45-$65	67	#4 Moonflower bowls	$25-$35	77	#5 - #9 mixing bowls	$30-$40
54	Eve-N-Bake casseroles	$20-$35	67	#24 Dogwood spaghetti bowl	$75-$100	77	#15 black on white pitcher	NA
54	Eve-N-Bake domed casseroles	$30-$45	67	Old style #18 Dogwood casserole	$135-$175	78	#07 nappy, special colors	$100-$200
54	Eve-N-Bake lug casseroles	$35-$50	68	#31 Dogwood platter	$135-$175	78	#39 spaghetti bowls, special colors	$150-$250
55	Eve-N-Bake mixing bowls	$20-$25	68	#42 Dogwood plate	$50-$75	78	#24 spaghetti bowl, special colors	$125-$200
55	Mixing bowls, blue/white bands	$20-$25	68	Old style Cross-Hatch pitcher	$125-$150	78	#39 spaghetti bowl, orange/brown	$300 est.
55	Casserole, blue/white bands	$30-$40	68	#16 Cross-Hatch pitcher	$240 **	79	#505 tea pot	$3300 **
55	#21 cookie jar, blue/white	$85-$125	68	#15 Cross-Hatch pitcher	$300 **	79	#115 coffee server	$3300-$3650 **
55	Old style pitcher, blue/white bands	$75-$100	68	#21 Cross-Hatch cookie jar	$200-$300	79	#112 tea pot	$2000-$2750 **
55	Deep mixing bowls	$25-$35	68	#18 groove handle casserole	$135-$175	80	#62 creamers	$90-$120
56	Mixing bowls	$20-$35	68	#40 Cross-Hatch cup	$90-$120	80	#98 sugar bowl, open	$150-$200
56	#1 bowl	$20-$30	69	#39 Cross-Hatch spaghetti bowl	$425 **	80	#98 sugar bowl, covered	$325-$400
57	#48 Rio Rose stacking set	$75-$120 ea..	69	#31 Cross-Hatch platter	$150-$200	80	#701 mugs	$400-$550 **
57	Oval handled casserole	$75-$90	69	#33 Cross-Hatch pie plate	$260 **	80	#501 mugs	$300-$350
57	8" casserole	$50-$75	69	#43 Cross-Hatch plate	$150 est.	80	#121 mugs	$175-$225
58	Mixing bowls	$25-$45	69	Cross-Hatch mixing bowls	$40-$60	80	#15 pitcher	$65-$85
58	8" baker	$45-$60	70	#43 & #42 Daisy plates	$50-$75	80	#16 pitcher	$90-$120
58	Rio Rose & Raised Rose pitchers	$120-$150	70	Daisy pie plate	$135-$175	80	#17 plain lip pitcher	$250-$275

PAGE	DESCRIPTION	VALUE
80	#17 ice-lip pitcher	$200-$225
80	#69 pitcher	$400-$500
80	#701 mug	$400-$550 **
80	#62 salesman sample	$200-$250
81	#117, #118 shakers, S & P holes	$100-$135 ea.
81	#117, #118 shakers, raised letters	$110-$150 ea.
81	#45 and #46 shakers	$225-$250 ea.
81	#126 cruets	$2500 pair **
81	#126 salesman sample cruets	$3000 est.
81	#31 salesman sample platter	$600 est.
81	#17 salesman sample ice-lip pitcher	$350 est.
81	Divided dinner plate	$1200 est.
82	#49 chop plate	$375-$450
82	#31 platter	$300-$400
82	#101 plate	$700 est.
82	#29 plate w/adv	$450-$600 **
82	#29 salesman sample plate	$750 est.
83	#49 plate w/adv	$500 est.
83	#29 plate w/adv	$450-$600 **
83	#18 tab handle & groove handle	$175-$250
83	#18 tab handle, #01 lid	$175-$250
83	#18 French handle, blade knob	$225-$275
83	#8182 2-leaf canister set	$450-$550 ea.
83	#8182 3-leaf canister set	$600 ea. est
84	#18 French handle, button knob	$200-$250
84	#72 canisters	$500-$625
84	#01 grease jar	$275-$325
84	#82 canister	$500-$600
84	#47 grease jar	$400-$500
84	#80 3-leaf cheese crock	$900-$1200
84	#91 cookie jars	$900-$1200
85	#02 refrigerator set	$1500 est.
85	#85 rectangular baker	$1200-$1600
85	#84 square covered baker	$1750-$2000
85	#21 cookie jar	$275-$375
85	#76 bean pots	$175-$225
85	#503 cookie jar	$425-$500
86	#502 bean pot	$900 **
86	#76 bean pot	$175-$225
86	#59 ice buckets	$225-$325
86	#1219 chip-n-dip w/rack	$300-$350
86,87	#0596 & #6012 chip-n-dip w/rack	$200-$250
87	#66, #67 covered bakers	$125-$150
87	#3/19 casserole	$175-$225
87	#2/48 casserole	$175-$225
87	#600, #601 covered bakers	$125-$150
87	#20 roaster	$1500-$2000
88	#70 Dutch oven	$275-$325
88	#110 covered baker	$200-$250
88	#133 electric warmer	$600-$800
88	#96 covered bakers	$100-$125
88	#3/19 boxed set with warmer	$500 est.
88	#73 covered bowl, Apple decoration	$180-$225
88	#73 covered bowl, banded decoration	$180-$225
89	#73 salad bowl	$75-$85
89	#74 salad bowl	$35-$40
89	#23 bowl	$100-$125
89	8" baker	$150-$175
90	#39 spaghetti bowl	$100-$175
90	#25 spaghetti bowl	$200-$225
90	#24 spaghetti bowl	$135-$185
90	#44 flat soup, inside band	$425-$475
90	#44 flat soup, outside band	$150-$175
90	#24 spaghetti bowl	$135-$185
90	#39 straight side spaghetti bowl	$135-$175
91	#50 bowl	$300-$350
91	2 & 3-leaf mixing bowls	$40-$60
92	#63 - #65 deep bowls	$80-$90
92	#106 salad bowl	$450-$590 **
92	#04 - #07 nappies	$30-$60
92	Ribbed mixing bowls	$60-$70
92	#33 pie plate	$110-$135
93	#63 - #65 deep bowls	$80-$90
93	#94 - #96 bakers	$45-$65
93	#60 bowl	$85-$100
93	#66, #67 bowls	$50-$70
93	#600, #601 bakers	$75-$90
93	#602 - #604 bakers & #1 bowl	$125-$150
93	#75 bean cup	$400-$650 **
93	#110 Open Apple covered baker	$300-$400
93	#96 Open Apple covered baker	$350-$450
94	#61 Reduced Apple deep bowl	$135-$150
94	#63- #65 Reduced Apple deep bowls	$80-$90
94	#74 Reduced Apple bowl	$35-$50
95	#62 Open Apple creamer	$900-$1200 **
95	#04 - #07 Open Apple nappies	$125-$200
95	Open Apple mixing bowls	$100-$125
95	#39 Open Apple spaghetti bowl	$900-$1000
95	#73 Open Apple salad bowl	$150-$200
96	#31 Silhouette platter	$125-$150
96	#18 Silhouette casserole	$80-$120
97	#15 Silhouette pitcher	$125-$175
97	#16 Silhouette pitcher	$80-$100
97	#17 Silhouette pitcher	$150-$175
97	#21 Silhouette cookie jar	$175-$200
97	#4 Silhouette bowl	$20-$25
97	#52 - #54 Silhouette bakers	$125-$150
97	Silhouette mixing & #52 Cherry bowls	$25-$35 ea.
98	#31 Cherry platter	$120-$140
98	#15 Cherry pitcher	$125-$150
98	#16 Cherry pitcher	$100-$135
98	#17 Cherry pitcher	$200-$250
98	#56 Cherry tumbler	$400 est
98	#45 Cherry salt shaker	$90-$110
98	#46 Cherry pepper shaker	$500 est.
99	#2/48 Cherry casserole	$135-$150
99	#53, #54 Cherry covered bakers	$120-$130
99	Boxed popcorn set	$800 est.
99	#55 Cherry bowl	$75-$90
100	#52 - #54 Cherry bakers	$25-$35
100	#39 Cherry spaghetti bowl	$110-$135
100	#24 Cherry spaghetti bowl	$100-$125
100	#18 Cherry groove handle casserole	$150-$200
100	#49 Cherry platter	$150-$175
100	#25 Cherry spaghetti bowl	$125-$150
101	#31 Cherry platter	$120-$140
101	#49 Cherry platter w/unusual flower	NA.
101	#21 Cherry cookie jar	$225-$275
102	#62 Rooster creamer	$175-$225
102	#98 Rooster sugar, open	$150-$225
102	#98 Roster sugar, covered	$450-$500
102	#117 and #118 Rooster shakers	$135-$190 ea.
102	#45 and #46 Rooster shakers	$200-$225 ea.
103	#62 Rooster creamer	$175-$275
103	#15 & #16 Rooster pitchers	$125-$150
103	#69 Rooster pitcher	$450-$600
103	#61 Rooster mug	NA
103	#80 Rooster cheese crock	$600-$900
103	#18 French handle casserole	$175-$275
103	#59 Rooster ice bucket	$250-$350
103	#76 Rooster cookie jar	$300-$375
103	#86 oval casserole	$1400 **
103	#85 rectangular baker	$800-$1000
104	#66, #67 Rooster bakers	$150-$225
104	#05 Rooster nappy	$175-$225
104	#70 Rooster Dutch oven	$225-$275
104	#39 Rooster spaghetti bowl	$325-$375
104	#33 Rooster pie plate	$300-$400
105	#60 - #67 bowls	$85-$150
105	Rooster mixing bowls	$75-$90
105	#63 - #65 Rooster deep bowls	$90-$120
105	#58 Rooster fruit bowl	$350 est.
106	Divided dinner plate	$800-$900
106	#45, #46 Dutch Tulip shakers	$500-$600 ea.
106	#69 Dutch Tulip pitcher	$500-$625
106	#16 Dutch Tulip pitcher	$150-$200
106	#15 Dutch Tulip pitcher	$130-$175
106	#62 Dutch Tulip creamer	$200-$250
107	#61 Dutch Tulip mug	NA
107	#85 Dutch Tulip rect. baker	$1000 est.
107	#8182 Dutch Tulip canister set	$500-$600 ea.
107	#76 Dutch Tulip cookie jar	$275-$350
107	#59 Dutch Tulip ice bucket	$400-$600
107	#80 Dutch Tulip cheese crock	$500-$900
108	#72 Dutch Tulip canister	$600 est.
108	#18 French handled casserole	$250-$350
108	#39 Dutch Tulip spaghetti bowl	$400-$450
108	#74 Dutch Tulip bowl, variation	$375 **
108	#66, #67 covered bakers	$225-$250
108	#60 - #68 Dutch Tulip bakers	$85-$125
109	#63 - #65 Dutch Tulip deep bowls	$90-$110
109	#73 Dutch Tulip salad bowl	$275-$350
110	#76 Bean pot w/decorated lid	$150-$200
110	#69 Tear Drop pitcher	$475-$525
110	#16 Tear Drop pitcher	$100-$150
110	#15 Tear Drop pitcher	$50-$60
110	#62 Tear Drop creamer	$175-$225
110	#117 and #118 Tear Drop shakers	$125-$200 ea.
110	#45 and #46 Tear Drop shakers	$125-$150 ea.
111	#76 Tear Drop bean pot	$75-$90
111	#75 Tear Drop bean cups	$15-$20
111	#76 bean pot, yellow glaze	$200 est.
111	#75 bean cup, yellow glaze	$25-$35 est.
111	#04 - #07 Tear Drop nappies	$30-$45
111	#05 Tear Drop covered nappy	$150-$170
112	#73 Tear Drop salad bowl	$125-$150
112	#74 Tear Drop salad bowl	$30-$40
112	#59 Tear Drop ice bucket	$325-$375
112	#84 Tear Drop square baker	$800-$900 est.
112	#60 - #68 Tear Drop bakers	$40-$60
112	#39 Tear Drop spaghetti bowl	$150-$175
113	#18 French handle casserole	$225-$275
113	#85 Tear Drop rectangular baker	$700-$900 **
113	Tear Drop mixing bowls	$40-$50
113	#63 - #65 deep bowls	$40-$65
113	#81 and #82 Tear Drop canisters	$275-$325
113	#72 Tear Drop canister	$400-$500
114	#97 Morning Glory creamer	$350-$650 **
114	#96 Morning Glory pitcher	$250-$300
114	#98 Morning Glory sugar bowl	$175-$275
114	#98 yellow Morning Glory sugar	$200-$250
114	#97 yellow Morning Glory creamer	$350-$650
114	Morning Glory mixing bowls	$90-$100
115	#94 Morning Glory baker	$300-$375
115	Yellow mixing bowls	$75-$85
115	#95 Morning Glory cookie jar	$400-$500
116	#505 A. Foliage tea pot	$2150 **
117	#115 A. Foliage open carafe	$150-$250
117	#17 A. Foliage ice-lip pitcher	$175-$225
117	#16 A. Foliage pitcher	$80-$100
117	#15 A. Foliage pitcher	$60-$80
117	#62 A. Foliage creamer	$175-$225
117	#110 A. Foliage covered baker	$125-$150
117	#112 A. Foliage tea pot	$1800 est.
117	#501 A. Foliage mugs	$125-$175
117	#121 A. Foliage mugs	$175-$225
118	#98 A. Foliage sugar bowl, open	$125-$175
118	#98 A. Foliage sugar bowl, covered	$300-$325
118	#62 A. Foliage creamer	$175-$225
118	#1219 A. Foliage chip-n-dip set	$200-$275
118	#117, #118 shakers, S & P holes	$90-$120 ea.
118	#117, #118 shakers, raised letters	$90-$120 ea.
118	#126 A. Foliage cruets	$350-$500 pair
118	#96 A. Foliage covered baker	$100-$120
118	#131 A. Foliage covered baker	$200-$225
118	#133 A. Foliage electric base	$350-$400
118	#506 A. Foliage fondue casserole	$250-$300
119	#02 A. Foliage stacking set	$900-$1200
119	#01 A. Foliage grease jar	$200-$225
119	#59 A. Foliage ice bucket	$225-$275
119	#133 A. Foliage non-electric base	$500 est.
119	#106 A. Foliage salad bowl	$80-$90
119	#503 A. Foliage cookie jar	$275-$350
119	#76 A. Foliage cookie jar	$125-$160
120	#31 A. Foliage platter	$125-$150
120	#04 - #07 A. Foliage nappies	$30-$40
120	#94 - #96 A. Foliage bakers	$35-$50
120	#39 A. Foliage spaghetti bowl	$125-$150
120	#33 A. Foliage pie plate	$135-$160
120	#73 A. Foliage salad bowls	$90-$100
121	#63 - #65 deep mixing bowls	$40-$50
121	A. Foliage mixing bowls	$30-$45
122	#503 Double Apple cookie jar	$350-$400
122	#76 Double Apple bean pot	$300-$450
122	#62 Double Apple creamer	$425-$600
122	#15 Double Apple pitcher	$350-$400
122	#16 Double Apple pitcher	$225-$300
123	Double Apple chip-n-dip set	$400-$500
123	#96 Double Apple covered baker	$275-$300
123	#04 Double Apple nappy	$85-$100
123	#05 - #07 Double Apple nappies	$35-$50
123	#63 - #65 Double Apple deep bowls	$60-$75
123	#73 Double Apple salad bowl	$100-$150
124	#503 Tulip cookie jar	$375-$450
124	#39 Tulip spaghetti bowl	$375-$425
124	Small bowl, blue band	NA
125	#63 - #65 Tulip deep mixing bowls	$85-$100
125	#600, #601 Tulip bakers	$120-$140
125	#602 - #604 Tulip bakers	$150-$275
125	#600, #601 Tulip covered bakers	$175-$250
125	#73 Tulip salad bowl	$250-$300
125	#62 Tulip creamer	$200-$275
125	#15 Tulip pitcher	$500-$600
125	#16 Tulip pitcher	$150-$200
125	#17 Tulip pitcher	$225-$300
126	#16 & #69 Butterfly pitcher	NA
126	#62 Butterfly creamer	NA
126	#76 Butterfly cookie jar & #67 baker	NA
127	#17 pitcher, Esmond apple	$350-$500 **
127	#31 mug, Esmond apple	$150-$250
128	Wooden carousel/warmer set	$1000 est.
128	#17 pitcher, Esmond grape	$350-$500 **
128	#31 mugs, fruit patterns	$150-$250
129	#36 Esmond apple & pear cookie jar	$85-$100
129	#34 Esmond apple & pear cookie jar	$75-$90
129	#62 Esmond fruit lazy susan set	$175-$200
129	#32 Esmond fruit lazy susan set	$100-$135
129	#73 Esmond apple & pear salad bowl	$100-$125
129	#31 Esmond apple & pear platter	$200-$225
129	#37 Esmond apple & pear casserole	$125-$200
130	#30 square canister	$180 ea.**
130	#37 shaded brown casserole	$50-$75
130	#36 shaded brown cookie jar	$60-$80
130	#75 shaded brown bean cup	$5-$10
130	#63 - #65 deep bowls, fruits	$85-$100
130	#34 happy/sad cookie jar	$250-$350
131	Small bowls	$35-$50
131	#16 casserole	$125-$175
131	#17 shaded brown pitcher	$135-$150
131	#31 shaded brown mugs	$25-$40
131	#701 shaded brown mugs	$30-$45
131	#61 & #16 shaded brown mugs	$25-$40 ea.
131	#34 shaded brown cookie jar	$40-$60
131	#31 shaded brown platter	$50-$75
132	#17 spray brown pitcher	$135-$150
132	#701 spray brown mugs	$30-$50
132	#62 spray brown creamer	$400 est.
132	#32 shaded brown canister set	$75-$100
134	#17 Eagle ice-lip pitcher	$375-$450
134	#72 Eagle cookie jar	$700-$900
134	#601 covered bakers	$225-$300
134	#59 Eagle ice bucket	$500-$600 est.
135	#76 Eagle cookie jar	$500-$600 est.
135	#601 covered bakers	$225-$300
135	Eagle mixing bowls	$135-$175
135	#59 & #72 Goodies jar	$300-$400 ea.
135	#76 Goodies jar	$200-$275
136	Snack set	$100-$150 ea.
136	#76 Goodies jar, script lettering	$350 est.
136	#603 Mexican motif bowl	$40-$50

PAGE	DESCRIPTION	VALUE
136	#601 Mexican motif bowl	$10-$15
137	#17 Corn Row pitcher	$125-$150
137	#16 Corn Row pitcher	$50-$60
137	#15 Corn Row pitcher	$135-$175
137	#15 pitcher, clear glaze w/adv.	$175-$200
138	#21 Corn Row cookie jars	$150-$200
138	Corn Row mixing bowls	$25-$35
138	Corn Row casseroles	$50-$75
138	Corn Row nappies	$30-$40
138	Corn Row custard cup	$30-$35
139	#21 Kolor Kraft cookie jar	$100-$125
139	#56 Kolor Kraft tumbler	$50-$75
139	#17 Kolor Kraft pitcher	$120-$150
139	#16 Kolor Kraft pitcher	$30-$45
139	#15 Kolor Kraft pitcher	$75-$100
139	Kolor Kraft covered bakers	$40-$60
140	#5 - #9 Kolor Kraft mixing bowls	$15-$30
140	#9 Kolor Kraft covered bowl	$50-$75
140	#52 - #54 Kolor Kraft bakers	$20-$35
140	#4 Kolor Kraft mixing bowl	$50 est.
141	#101 cookie jar, yellow	$125-$150
141	#101 cookie jar, blue	$150-$225
142	#101 cookie jar, green	$125-$150
142	#101 cookie jar, pink	$150-$225
142	#100 Basket Weave salad bowl	$20-$30
142	#102 Basket Weave salad bowl	$10-$15
143	Boxed Basket Weave salad set	$100-$125
143	#99 Basket Weave covered baker	$50-$75
143	#127 Basket Weave refrigerator jars	$50-$75
143	Basket Weave plates & saucers	$15-$35
144	Basket Weave mixing bowls	$20-$30
144	#810 Heirloom pitcher	$75-$110
144	#806 Heirloom mug	$20-$25
144	#801 JC Stoneware mug	$25-$35
144	#801 Heirloom mug	$20-$25
145	#812 Heirloom bean pot	$75-$95
145	#816 Heirloom bean cups	$5-$10
145	#806 JC Stoneware bowl	$20-$30
145	#100 Basket Weave bowl	$20-$30
145	#102 Basket Weave bowl	$10-$15
145	#800 JC Stoneware cookie jar	$100-$125
145	#811 Heirloom cookie jar	$100-$125
146	#803 bowl	$20-$30
146	#807 bowl	$10-$15
146	#815 casserole	$35-$45
146	#814 casserole	$15-$20
146	#803 JC Stoneware casserole	$20-$25
146	#802 casserole	$25-$30
147	#805 JC Stoneware baker	$20-$25
147	#808 covered baker	$25-$30
147	#803 JC Stoneware casserole	$20-$25
147	#808 JC Stoneware cup	$30-$40
147	#802 Heirloom bowl	$25-$30
147	#808 Heirloom Baker	$25-$30
147	Heirloom mixing bowls	$20-$30
148	#201 - #204 Owens canisters	$135-$175 ea.
150	#201 - #204 Owens canisters	$135-$175 ea.
150	Owens mixing bowls	$30-$40
151	#207 Owens cookie jar	$200-$250
151	Owens deep mixing bowls	$35-$45
151	#205 Owens baker	$30-$45
152	#200C Owens covered baker	$50-$75
152	#608C covered baker	$60-$75
152	#617W cookie barrel	$85-$125
152	#618W bean pot	$90-$125
153	#613W - #615W pitchers	$50-$100
153	#626W, #627W shakers	$75-$90 ea..
153	#605W - #610W mixing bowls	$20-$30
153	#608C covered baker	$60-$75
154	#612W bowl	$20-$25
154	#605W - #610W bowls	$20-$30
154	#611W bowl	$25-$40
155-9	Prices are without bases. Add $25.00 for bases.	
	"Lemonade" kegs, yellow	$90-$100
	"Iced Tea" keg, 3 gallon	$125-$150
	"Iced Tea" kegs, brown, russet, gold	$65-$85
	"Iced Tea" kegs, other colors	$100-$125
	Kegs w/trade names, brown, russet, gold	$120-$135
	Kegs w/trade names, other colors	$150-$175
161	Kathy Kale test pieces	NA
161-2	Kathy Kale tea pots & coffee servers	$500 est. ea.
162	Kathy Kale dinner plate	$35-$50
162	Kathy Kale cup & saucer	$65-$85
162	Kathy Kale serving platter	$75-$100
162	Kathy Kale deep pie dish	$50-$60
162	Kathy Kale mixing bowls	$15-$25
163	Kathy Kale shakers & casserole	$100-$125 ea.
163	Kathy Kale creamer & covered sugar	$75-$100 ea.
163	Kathy Kale custard cup & salad bowls	$15-$25
164	Kathy Kale coffee cup	$50-$70
164	Kathy Kale party mug	$35-$45
165	#15 pitcher & #62 creamer, brown/white	$75-$150
165	#16 pitcher, brown/white	$35-$60
166	#69 pitcher, brown/white	$200-$300
166	#62 creamers	$75-$150
166	#132 carafe	$125-$175
167	#15 pitchers	$75-$100
167	#16 pitchers	$35-$60
167	#60 bowl	$20-$25
167	#61 mug	$35-$50

PAGE	DESCRIPTION	VALUE
167	#18 tab handle casserole	$60-$100
167	#101 plate	$40-$60
168	#121 mug	$45-$75
168	#59 ice bucket	$90-$135
168	#84 square casserole	$75-$100
169	#130 with soup tureen lid	$75-$100
169	#133 electric base	$125-$150
169	#131 covered bowl	$40-$75
169	#85 rectangular baker	$30-$45
170	#96 covered bakers	$50-$75
170	#133 electric base	$125-$150
170	#130 with soup tureen lid	$75-$100
170	#1219 chip-n-dip set	$85-$120
170	#506 casserole	$75-$100
170	#54 covered baker	$35-$50
171	#58 fruit bowl	$20-$30
171	#74, #60 bowls	$10-$20
171	#18 French casserole	$75-$100
171	#73, #74 salad bowls	$10-$25
171	#63 - #65 deep bowls	$30-$45
172	#59 ice bucket, Black Beauty	$150-$200
172	#17 pitcher, Black Beauty	$135-$175
172	#56 tumblers, Black Beauty	$100-$400 **
172	#52, #55 salad bowls	$20-$35
173	#54 covered baker w/stand	$85-$125
173	#53, #54 covered bakers	$45-$60
173	#49 grease jar	$200-$300
174	#58 fruit bowl, Black Beauty	$30-$40
174	#45, #46 shakers, Greenbriar	$150 ea. est.
174	#52, #55 Greenbriar bowls	$25-$40
174	#54 baker, Greenbriar	$50-$75
175	#18 casserole, Greenbriar	$75-$100
175	#17 pitcher, Greenbriar	$135-$175
175	#56 tumblers, Greenbriar	$85-$300 **
175	#39 spaghetti bowl, Greenbriar	$50-$75
175	Mixing bowls, Greenbriar	$25-$40
175	#55 salad bowl, Greenbriar	$25-$35
175	#75 bean cups, Greenbriar	$20-$25
176	#117, #118 shakers, Nassau	$25-$35 ea.
176	#126 cruets, Nassau	$90-$120 set
176	#106 salad bowl, Nassau	$20-$30
176	#120 bowl, Nassau	$10-$15
176	#110 casserole, Nassau	$45-$60
177	#15 pitcher, green/white	$150-$175
177	#16 pitcher, green/white	$75-$100
177	#58 bowl, blue/white	$35-$50
177	$60 bowl, blue/white	$15-$25
178	#115 carafe, blue/cobalt	$125-$175
179	#115 carafe, teal/black	$125-$175
180	#117, #118 shakers	$85-$125 ea.
180	#31 platter, teal/black	$75-$100
180	10" plate, teal/black	$40-$70
180	#73 bowl, pink/white	$35-$50
180	#74 bowl, pink/white	$15-$25
181	#58 bowl, pink/white icing	$60-$85
181	#54 baker pink/black	$75-$90
181	#58 fruit bowl, pink/black	$50-$75
181	#59 ice buckets, pink/black	$135-$175
182	#60 bowl, pink/black	$20-$30
182	#96 covered baker, Westwood	$50-$70
182	#1219 chip-n-dip set, Westwood	$90-$100
182	#16 pitcher, brown/cream	$75-$100
182	#59 ice bucket, brown/cream	$135-$175
183	#88, #89 bowls, brown/cream	$25-$40
183	#54 covered baker, brown/cream	$50-$75
183	#86 oval casserole, brown/cream	$100-$135
184	#117, #118 shakers, K. Queen	$100 ea. est.
184	#66, #67 covered bakers, K. Queen	$85-$100
184	#600, #601, #110 bakers, K. Queen	$85-$100
185	5" - 14" mixing bowls, K. Queen	$20-$40
185	#616 mixing bowl, K. Queen	$60-$85
186	#17 pitcher, K. Queen	$150-$175
186	#01 grease jar, K. Queen	$300 est.
186	#59 ice bucket, K. Queen	$150-$175
186	#503 cookie jar, K. Queen	$150-$175
186	#76 cookie jar, K. Queen	$125-$150
186	5" - 9" ribbed mixing, K. Queen	$25-$35
187	#600 - #604 bakers, K. Queen	$30-$50
187	#63 - #65 deep bowls	$30-$40
187	Various bowls, K. Queen	$20-$35
188	#33 pie plate, K. Queen	$75-$90
188	#117, #118 shakers, Par-T-Que	$85-$100 ea.
188	#17 pitcher, Par-T-Que	$150-$180
1188	#62 creamer, Par-T-Que	$150-$200
188	#98 sugar, open	$90-$120
188	#98 sugar, covered	$200-$225
189	#112 tea pot, Par-T-Que	$650-$750
189	#115 coffee server, Par-T-Que	$700 est
189	#121 mug, Par-T-Que	$50-$75
189	#31 platter, Par-T-Que	$75-$90
189	#01 grease jar, Par-T-Que	$150-$225
190	#503 cookie jar, Par-T-Que	$175 est.
190	#101, #102 plates, Par-T-Que	$25-$40
190	#44 flat soup bowl, Par-T-Que	$35-$50
190	#63 - #65 bowls, Par-T-Que	$35-$50
191	#33 banded pie plates	$30-$50
191	5" - 14" banded bowls	$20-$35
191	#39 spaghetti bowls, inside bands	$75-$100
191	5" - 9" ribbed mixing bowls	$20-$35
192	Old style pitcher	$75-$100

PAGE	DESCRIPTION	VALUE
192	#17 pitcher	$135-$175
192	#75 bean cup, "Pa Dutch Days"	$35-$50
192	#59 ice bucket	$150-$200
192	#54 covered baker	$35-$50
192	5" - 9" mixing bowls	$20-$35
192-3	8" baker & #53 covered baker	$35-$50
193	#73 salad bowl	$25-$35
193	5" - 9" mixing bowls	$20-$35
194	10" dinner plates, pastel	$85-$100 est.
195	#15 pitcher, Brownstone	$75-$100
195	#16 pitcher, Brownstone	$30-$50
195	#17 pitcher, Brownstone	$135-$150
195	#117, #118 shakers, Brownstone	$60-$80 ea.
195	#01 grease jar, Brownstone	$125-$150
195	5" - 9" mixing bowls, Brownstone	$20-$30
195	#600 - #604 bakers, Brownstone	$20-$35
195	#600, #601 covered bakers	$50-$75
196	#17 pitcher, Brownstone	$135-$150
196	#121 mug, Brownstone	$60-$80
196	#62 creamer, Brownstone	$125-$200
196	#76 bean pot, Brownstone	$75-$85
196	#117, #118 shakers, Brownstone	$60-$80 ea.
196	#75 bean cup, Brownstone	$10-$20
196	#96 baker, Brownstone	$25-$40
196	shakers, raised letters, bisque	$50-$75 ea.
196	shakers, S & P holes, bisque	$15-$25 ea.
196	#126 cruets, bisque	$60-$85 pair
197	#1219 chip-n-dip set, bisque	$100-$125
197	Salad bowls, bisque	$5-$20
197	Boxed bean pot set	$85-$100
198	#63 - #65 bowls, bronze luster	$70-$85
198	#117, #118 shakers, bronze luster	$75-$90 ea.
198	#15 pitcher, bronze luster	$100-$150
198	#115 carafe, bronze luster	$300 est.
198	#600, #601 covered bakers	$75-$90
198	#49 plate, bronze luster	$45-$65
199	Lazy susan, black bowls	$150-$200
199	#115 carafes, various colors	$125-$175
200	#115 carafe	$125-$150
200	#69 pitchers	$100-$150
200	#501 mug, clear glaze	$65-$85
200	#501 mug w/adv.	$250 **
201	#101, #102 plates	$35-$45
201	#75 bean cup	$5
201	#75 covered cup	$35-$50
201	#77 bean cup	$10
201	#76 bean pot	$20-$25
201	#93 bean pot	$50-$60
201	#502 bean pot	$35-$50
202	#88, #89 bowls	$30-$45
202	#76 Campbell's Kids bean pot	$125-$175
202	Custard cup	$15-$25
202	#75 bean cup, yellow	$15-$25
202	5" - 9" mixing bowls, two-tone	$20-$35
203	Policeman cookie jar	$1500-$1800
204	Jack-O-Lantern	$2500 **
204	#100Z cracker jar	NA
205	#92 Bird Cage cookie jar	NA
206-208	7 1/2" custom plates	$100-$200 est.
209-211	Eva Zeisel ware	NA
212	Swirled bean pot set	$250 est.
212	#75 bean cup, Confetti	$50-$75
212	#18 casserole, Confetti	$125-$175
213	9" custom bowls	NA
214	Barrel bank	NA
214	#16 reduced tulip pitcher	$900 **
214	#16 sponged pitcher	$200
214	#15 crocus pitcher	NA
214	#15 Ivy pitcher	NA
215	#24 spaghetti bowl	NA
215	#101 plate, pastel rings	$200 **
215	Divided plate, rosebud	NA
215	#74 Fiesta bowl	$50-$75
215	#63 glaze sample	NA
216	#62 Christmas creamer	$800-$1200
216	#75 Christmas sugar bowl	$300-$400
216	Custom plates, mugs	NA
217	Custom plates, mugs	NA
217	#31, #14 Christmas punch set	$2500 **
218	Custom plates, bowls	NA
219	Chef shakers	$1300 **
219	Custom plates, bowls, mugs	NA
220	#69 pitcher, fruits	$325 **
220	Custom mugs, bowl, pitcher	NA
221	Bears, unmarked	$400 **
222	Chinese (?) bowls	$35-$50
222	#500 mug & Paperweight	NA
222	EZ-Mix bowl	$50-$75
223	Metal stands	$35-$100
224	300 series planters	$35-$75
224	Bud vases	$50-$100
225	900 series planters	$35-$75
225	150 series planters	$75-$100 est.
226	Mink dishes	$50-$75
226	Dog dishes	$40-$65
226	Kitty dishes	$75-$100
226	#62 kitten bowl	$35-$50
227	94B, 95B & Romar.y Spartan ash trays	$50-$75
227	#100 ash tray	$85-$100
227	Salesman sample ash tray	$125 est.
227	#90 knife sharpener	$200-$650 **